Husbands and Other Men I've Played With

Patricia Fox Sheinwold

Husbands
and Other Men
I've Played With

HOUGHTON MIFFLIN COMPANY BOSTON
1976

Chapter 6, "Blue Ribbon Baby," has
appeared in *Popular Bridge*.

The excerpt from "The Trouble with Women
Is Men" on page vii is reprinted by
permission of Little, Brown and Company
from *Verses from 1929 On* by Ogden Nash.
Copyright 1942 by The Curtis Publishing
Company.

Library of Congress Cataloging in Publication Data

Sheinwold, Patricia Fox.
   Husbands and other men I've played with.

1. Contract bridge. 2. Sheinwold, Patricia Fox.
I. Title.
GV1282.3.S4662   795.4'152   76–22661
ISBN 0–395–24779–9

Printed in the United States of America

C 10 9 8 7 6 5 4 3 2 1

friend is a six-letter word,
for Jeanne

Indeed, each time he transgresses, your chance of
correcting his faults grows lesser,
Because he produces either a maddeningly logical
explanation or a look of martyrdom which leaves you instead
of him feeling the remorse of the transgressor.
Such are husbandly foibles, but there are moments
when a foible ceases to be a foible.

— From *"The Trouble with Women Is Men,"* Ogden Nash

Thank You to:
Marion Horvitz who believed
Nathan Werter who encouraged
John Fernbach who advised
Joseph Kolker who enlightened
Richard Freeman who tightened
Jacques de Spoelberch who accepted
Daphne A. Ehrlich who agreed

Contents

Husbands
and Other Men
I've Played With

1—

A Fish and
Mister Fisher

"I HATE YOU. I never want to see you again."

Pretty strong words from a twenty-year-old to a forty-year-old who was neither her father nor her lover. Just a bridge partner.

It wasn't the first time I had felt like a fool at the card table, but it was the first and last time I acted foolish in front of other people at the card table.

Worse still, I jumped up, fled from the table, and ran outside, the tears streaming (both actions frowned upon by the tournament bridge–playing populace). But I was young, humiliated, and confused. Unknowingly, I had made a horrible mistake in the bidding, the opponents had snickered, and a roomful of people had turned to gape as my partner screeched, "How *could* you make a bid like that?" And there was, too, the score, which read *minus* 1500 for our side. Even Secretariat couldn't beat such a parlay.

I stood on the sidewalk, sobbing. Mr. Irvin Fisher of Baltimore, Maryland (previously referred to as my partner), appeared and offered me his handkerchief.

"Why did you ask me to play?" I wailed.

"Because you're talented. But you're also a beginner and inexperienced in tournament play."

"I've played for years — you know that. Remember how we met?"

"We met because your husband was late for our regular game and you offered to sit in. And that's when I recognized your innate talent for bridge."

"And now my innate talent is spilling all over the sidewalk."

I moved away as people from the game were glancing in our direction. "See what you've done. I'm so embarrassed, I could die." The tears started flowing again.

"Pat, do you want to be a good bridge player?"

His tone was quietly sincere and so genuinely serious that I interrupted my crying for the moment and sat down on the scrubbed white marble street stoop that's typical of Baltimore's rowhouses. "I think so, Irvin."

"Well, if you want to be, I can teach you to be. But I must be able to teach you at the table, and you must be able to take instruction without embarrassment right then and there. Not criticism — instruction. There's a big difference."

"I know that, but the onlookers don't."

"I promise you that six months from now you'll be playing rings around those people laughing in there. They'll probably be asking you to play."

"But why do you have to do it at the table? It makes me uncomfortable."

"Because until you are expert enough to remember all the hands, I must drive home the point at the proper time." He smiled. "Before you make another error."

"Thanks a lot, she said."

"Bridge is a game of mistakes. The person who makes the fewest emerges the winner. It's as simple as that."

"Apparently, I didn't make such a simple mistake, the way you said —"

"*Said,* Pat, not yelled. That's the key word. Yellers never hear each other. I want you to hear me."

"I think I understand what you're saying . . . A big ego gets in the way of listening, and if we don't listen, we don't learn."

"True. If you can handle this, you will learn. How you handle the yellers is something else for you to work out."

"You're throwing a lot at me" (tossing him his drenched hankie), "but I've made three decisions. One, I'll never cry over bridge again. Two, I do want to learn from you, and three, I can't walk into that room again tonight."

"And four," said Irv, "you've just undone one and two."

"You mean, I have to go back?"

"If you believe what I told you."

I walked back into that snickering lion's den with my Daniel trailing me. We sat down to play the second hand against the same opponents. They lost no time in sticking the score from the previous hand under my nose. "Sign it," they said. It was painful, but I initialed it by the minus 1500 points — crunching the pencil and the insides of my cheeks simultaneously. Irvin Fisher kept his eyes carefully glued to his cards, his mouth shut. I picked up the cards and was delighted to open the following thirteen gems:

Spades: Ace King
Hearts: Ace King 10 8 6 5 2
Diamonds: Ace 4
Clubs: 10 4

Bidding:

Me	Opponent	Irv	Opponent
2 Hearts	Pass	3 Hearts	Pass
3 Spades*	Pass	4 Clubs*	Pass
4 Diamonds*	Pass	5 Diamonds*	Pass
7 Notrump	Pass	Pass	Pass

All Vulnerable
Opening Lead: 5 of Spades

* All cue bids.

I guess I should have been content with 6 Notrump, but I'm an overbidder, which beats being a yeller. Irv put his cards down and there it was — *6 Notrump*, all cozy and warm. Not 7. To hide my horror I pretended to be looking for something I had dropped on the floor. Actually, I was looking for the thirteenth trick. My thoughts went something like this.

I'll go down one trick, and he'll say, "Could you really count thirteen tricks?" And I'll say, "But I wasn't doubled," and he'll say, "What's that got to do with it?" And I'll say, "But I thought I had a good play for seven," and he'll say, "You had a good play for six" and "We don't play seven when six is a good thing." And the opponents will laugh again. And the roomful of people will turn to gape again. And I'll flee again. And the damn score will have to be signed again.

And then I thought, what the hell has all that got to do with bridge? Nothing. Absolutely nothing! As I sat upright again, Irv asked, "Did you find what you were looking for?" Find it I did, and I never lost it again.

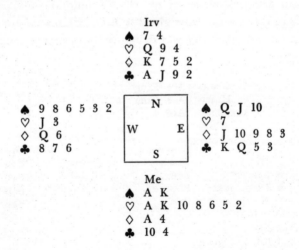

```
                        Irv
                    ♠  7 4
                    ♡  Q 9 4
                    ◇  K 7 5 2
                    ♣  A J 9 2

♠ 9 8 6 5 3 2      ┌─────────┐      ♠ Q J 10
♡ J 3              │    N    │      ♡ 7
◇ Q 6              │ W     E │      ◇ J 10 9 8 3
♣ 8 7 6            │    S    │      ♣ K Q 5 3
                   └─────────┘
                        Me
                    ♠  A K
                    ♡  A K 10 8 6 5 2
                    ◇  A 4
                    ♣  10 4
```

I started studying the hand. The opponents feigned interest in the dummy, but I could tell by their faces that I had fallen on mine. If I were going down, they were going to have to work to set me. I decided to cash all my high cards, thus setting up all theirs, then run the Hearts and hope they would discard incorrectly. I won the opening Spade lead and in this order cashed the King of Spades, the Ace of Diamonds, and the Ace of Clubs. I started pulling Hearts with the Queen in dummy and crossed to my hand to continue. (The seasoned player will recognize exactly what I was about, but for me at that time, instinct was stronger than skill.)

When I played the fifth Heart I noticed my right-hand opponent. He was playing slower and seemed to have a problem. On the sixth Heart he began to thrash about in his chair. On the seventh Heart he was rendered helpless. Did you hear that? *Helpless.*

Here is the end position:

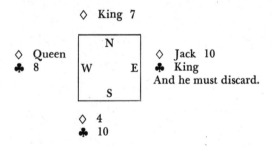

◇ King 7

◇ Queen   N   ◇ Jack 10
♣ 8   W   E   ♣ King
        S   And he must discard.

◇ 4
♣ 10

Seven Notrump bid and made. "Thank God," I murmured to myself.

"Very nice coup," cooed Irv.

"Innate I call it."

"Vienna is what we call it."

And that's how I stumbled into and executed what is famous in the world of bridge as a Vienna Coup. First, you set up the winning trick for the opponent, and then, make him throw it away by squeezing him.

In bed late that night, while waiting for sleep, I thought about Irv's words: "Be able to take constructive criticism at the table without embarrassment." Is that really possible, or is the ego too sensitive? Was this the vital clue to playing successfully with all kinds of people — ego? I wasn't sure, but I sure was going to try.

That tearful night when I walked back into the bridge room, I walked back into the world of bridge — for better or worse. That marriage, and a few husbands and other men I've played with, has lasted twenty-five years.

2—

The First Foursome

I STARTED PLAYING bridge in the kitchen. The regulars in the game were my father's employees: Karl (butler), his wife Lydia (cook), Mae (maid), and Kirby (chauffeur). In aggregate, they had worked for him a total of 120 years. It explains in part why they played bridge: bridge was my father's passionate pastime. Any Little Jack Horner who sat in the corner in *our* house was put there, you can be sure, because he failed to make 4 Hearts. So went my nursery rhymes, at least.

Day and night, sounds emanated from the living room where the standing game was held. These were expressions of glee, relief, complaint, and too often ones of disgust, with screams and an occasional door slamming. In time, the same sounds came from the kitchen, and neither room seemed to care or be aware of the other. However, if the living room knew what the kitchen said about its bidding, there would have been mass unemployment on the spot.

One bright sunny day I returned home early and hungry like the twelve-year-old that I was. I detoured past the game in the living room in favor of the pantry — and the sounds of the kitchen game. Mae was screeching, "Karl would never behave that way if he weren't married to Lydia." While carefully opening the fridge, I heard Kirby retort, "Precisely why there are no women in the boss's game." That was Kirby's affectionate name for my father. And after a few seconds he continued, "Now we don't have a fourth — just when I have a good hand." I had my hand on the dessert for the evening meal when they spied me. Now I was in for it! But instead of the usual "Oh no, you don't!" or "Can't you wait for dinner?" they simply looked at each other like three people suddenly plugged into one thought and said in unison, "Why not?" With that, I dropped the chocolate mousse.

Still no scolding. "Wanna be our fourth?" chirped Kirby. Mae and Lydia nodded in agreement. A fast survey of the situation produced from me a quick "Uh, huh," because right there at the table sat my meals, transportation, and laundry.

"Where's Karl?" I asked, as Kirby motioned me to sit down opposite Lydia, "and why is Lydia crying?"

Mae handed me a napkin to remove the mousse, Lydia wiped her eyes, and Kirby answered, "Cut the cards." And so my bridge life started.

At least I thought that's when it started. But according to my astrologer, I was conceived between 6 Hearts, doubled, bid, and made, and 4 Diamonds, doubled, making five. My parents were divorced between 6 Clubs, doubled, down four, and 7 Spades, doubled, down three. What else can be expected when one Leo marries another Leo? Some of their more practical friends reasoned that it was because their bidding was incompatible. One thing was certain: Notrump would be my favorite contract.

It took Lydia and Karl a long time to make up. In that time I played daily with the other three and struggled to learn the basic rules as quickly as possible. One thing was for sure — no one agreed on anything. Especially the stakes.

"I don't see how you can expect me to play for money on my allowance even if I knew how to play." This fell on six deaf ears. But their ears were just as deaf when it came to hearing each other at the table. This was where I put some twelve-year-old common sense to work. I had known these people all my life and to achieve my ends had had to learn how to get around them. If it worked at getting an extra piece of pie or a button sewed on a blouse ten minutes before I was to wear it, certainly the same strategy could be applied at the table. Until my knowledge increased and my skill developed I would have to rely on their character and personality traits to guide me. I wasn't aware at the time how important this was, but it proved to be then and now the necessary ingredient in partnership understanding.

Mae was born and raised in Scotland, and her built-in parsimonious nature took its place at the bridge table. She would never overbid. Once I recognized this trait and learned to compensate for it, we seldom failed to reach a game. She was a partner one could count on. Her bids were as reliable as the buttons she sewed on my blouse.

Lydia was as German as her apple strudel. She had come from the ship to our house and that was about as American as she ever became. She longed for the Fatherland, which was understandable. When World War II started she hovered between belligerency and some kind of blue funk. She couldn't believe this could happen in her Germany. At the card table she was shrewd, proud, and aggressive. (She could have started a war all by herself.) I had to be very cautious in bidding with her and never stick my neck out. Once she had decided on the final contract, nothing could change her mind, even if another would have been a sure thing. Years later I named my Mercedes Lydia. "Why such a funny name?" I was asked. "Because one day the car and I were on our way to the beach. Halfway, I changed my mind and decided to make a detour to shop. But the car had a mind of its own and wouldn't make the turn. It went directly to the beach with the driver screaming all the way." My answer may have sounded confusing, but I knew what I meant. Lydia always knew what her bids meant, but her partners were always slightly befuddled.

Kirby was 100 per cent American. He was friendly and loose, but he never let us forget that he was the only male in the game. He would do this by flexing his muscles instead of his brain. Much to my amazement, Lydia and Mae were constantly vying for his attention. If he thought about a cold beer, it suddenly appeared on the table. He had seniority over the others and certainly over me. I resented his authority and dreamed up ways to thwart him. But the bridge game began to work in my favor. Instead of having to ride the school bus home, I would find Kirby waiting for me with his bidding cap on. He had taken to instructing me in *his* bidding technique so I could have the jump on the other girls. It was devious, but it beat riding home in a rickety old bus.

Slowly I became adept at handling cards, and eventually my bank account showed it. But it was understanding their personalities that enabled me to win. How hard you work at the game is what determines how well you play, but how well you learn to handle yourself, your partners, and your opponents determines how consistently successful you are at the table. Bridge has always been and will always be a *partnership* game. If you prefer solo games, don't take up bridge!

I still remember the first game in Notrump that I bid and made — not because my memory is that fantastic, but because it was the first time I *consciously* discovered how to use my intuition at the bridge table.

I can't honestly say that I remember all the low cards, but I have filled them in as best I could. They don't really matter, as you'll see.

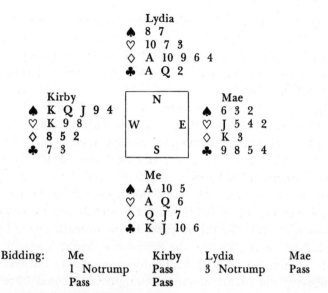

Lydia
♠ 8 7
♡ 10 7 3
♢ A 10 9 6 4
♣ A Q 2

Kirby
♠ K Q J 9 4
♡ K 9 8
♢ 8 5 2
♣ 7 3

Mae
♠ 6 3 2
♡ J 5 4 2
♢ K 3
♣ 9 8 5 4

Me
♠ A 10 5
♡ A Q 6
♢ Q J 7
♣ K J 10 6

Bidding:	Me	Kirby	Lydia	Mae
	1 Notrump	Pass	3 Notrump	Pass
	Pass	Pass		

Opening Lead: King of Spades

I held the South cards. I didn't have any special rules for my bidding, but opened the bidding with 1 Notrump. Years later, I discovered that this was the "book" bid for the hand, but at that stage who'd read a book?

Lydia was my partner. She didn't trust me to play the hand properly, especially since most inexperienced players flounder horribly at Notrump contracts, but she raised to 3 Notrump and hoped the hand would be a pianola. (We never hear this term anymore, but in the early days of contract bridge a hand was called a pianola if it practically played itself.)

Kirby held the West cards. He led the King of Spades with great confidence. I played a low Spade from the dummy, and Mae played the 2.

I wanted to take that first trick with the Ace of Spades, but I happened to look at Kirby out of the corner of my eye, and I could tell that he wanted me to win the trick. I can't explain how I knew, but I did.

Since Kirby was a far more experienced bridge player, I felt that I would be better off resisting what he wanted. So I played a low Spade, refusing to win the first trick.

Kirby had seen my hesitation and had no doubt where the Ace of Spades was. I remember that he gave me a strange look as he led a fierce Queen of Spades.

It was even clearer than it was before: Kirby wanted me to take my Ace. I had never been an obedient child, and I certainly didn't intend to start at the bridge table. If he wanted me to play the Ace of Spades, I wouldn't do it. So I played the 10.

Kirby gave me that same strange look and led the Jack of Spades, this time very calmly. Since I had no choice, I took the Ace.

The next play was easy. I had seen finesses, and I knew that I was supposed to develop tricks in my longest suit. (Years later I learned that there were times when it was wrong to finesse and also times when you didn't try to develop your longest suit. But that was ten years and a dozen partners later.)

At any rate, I led the Queen of Diamonds for a finesse. Mae took the King of Diamonds and naturally returned the 2 of Hearts.

I was tempted to play the Queen of Hearts as another finesse, but just in time I remembered to give Kirby that look out of the corner of my eye. He was trying to look nonchalant, but I was absolutely sure that he had the King of Hearts and wanted me to finesse.

I hadn't worked out the hand, mind you, but I was working out a principle that was to help me in all the bridge I have played since: *Playing your opponents is just as good as playing your cards.*

Kirby wanted me to finesse, therefore I decided not to play the Queen. I took the trick with the Ace of Hearts and began to take my tricks. Somewhat to my surprise, I found that I could take all the rest, making my contract with an overtrick.

One of the reasons I remember this hand so clearly is that there was so much talk afterward. Kirby was enough of a good sport to praise me for a "brilliant" play. Where had I learned the hold-up play, he wanted to know.

When it became clear that I didn't even know the name of the play, he was even more impressed. How could a twelve-year-old invent such a play all by herself! (For readers who don't play much bridge, Kirby praised my play because he would have defeated me if I had taken the first or second Spade trick; when Mae took the King of Diamonds she would be able to return a Spade. And, of course, he would have defeated me if I had tried the Heart finesse; he would have won with the King of Hearts and then have taken the rest of his Spades.)

I was afraid to tell him that I hadn't invented a play, but had discovered that I could tell what people wanted if I just relaxed and let myself absorb the atmosphere, the vibes. Can you imagine Kirby's face if I had told him that? "The atmosphere?" he'd shriek. "All you have to know about the atmosphere is whether or not to wear a raincoat." It amounts to the same thing, but he'd never understand.

After three months Lydia and Karl patched things up. She went on cooking and he went on butling, but at the drop of a pancake they would start arguing about why they were arguing. I don't know who finally settled the dispute, but three months later it certainly had nothing to do with bridge; it had a lot to do with ego.

I went back to algebra and the bus.

Eventually I won the United States Women's Team Bridge Championship. Lydia divorced Karl and married Kirby, and Mae married Karl. The last time I saw the four of them playing bridge together, Mae and Lydia were partners. I wonder if *they've* married by now?

3—

My Hearts (Spades, Diamonds, and Clubs) Belong to Daddy

LIBIDO: Why aren't you working on the chapter about your father?

ID: I am, sort of.

LIBIDO: It seems logical to me that the next chapter should take place in the living room. Isn't that where you continued your bridge-playing after you graduated from the kitchen?

ID: Yep.

LIBIDO: Well?

ID: I'm pleasure-seeking today. See how happy I am rolling around in this swimming pool filled with sky-blue water. Or maybe I'm floating in the sky filled with pool-blue water.

LIBIDO: Your ego got in the way last night when you failed to make that hand. Your father would have made it. He knew the King of Clubs was always singleton!

ID: With Daddy's luck he would have gotten a different lead. And besides, that's just another of those dumb sayings.

LIBIDO: Is that so?

ID: I'm afraid so. Daddy was the victim of a lot of bridge

clichés, and just like the King of Clubs always being alone, the others are wrong, wrong, wrong.

LIBIDO: Well, it was certainly your ego that made you play your way instead of his.

ID: It was my superego — you know, the conscience of my unconscious — that made me play it the right way.

LIBIDO: I think you'd better get to work on the next chapter.

With my psyche intact, the corporeal part of me went under the water in the huge swimming pool where the above conversation had taken place. Using a crab-type underwater stroke, I swam to the other end of the pool, where I collided with the King of Clubs.

"Hi," I gurgled, "are you alone?"

"Sure am," he answered. "Didn't your father tell you I'm always alone?"

"I think my father made it up. Most of the time you're not a singleton." I swam away, but could see by his reflection he was following me. "It was just another one of his crazy sayings," I continued.

"Is that so. What other sayings don't you believe?"

"Well, for instance, how about 'The Queen lies over the Jack'? That's really a doozy."

Without answering he made a quick turn, took a few strokes, and slithered into the drain. I followed, and much to my surprise went down the drain after him. The water propelled us along until we plopped into a large, bright room pregnant with Kings, Queens, and Jacks all busily engaged in conversation. I felt ridiculous in a purple bikini with my hair tied in pigtails. To the right was a jury box and in front of me, a high platform with a single chair.

This is no tea party, I mused to myself. I think I'm in court.

On cue a Joker entered, assuming the role of a bailiff, and banged for order. The Honor cards took their seats in the jury box and the Ace of Spades, wearing his usual black garb, entered to the Joker's announcement: "This court will now come to order."

"Patricia Fox, you are now charged with disobedience toward your elders. How do you plead?" the Spade Ace addressed me.

"Your Honor, and I do mean Your Honor, I will plead my own case, but I'm not sure what I'm pleading."

He picked up a bridge score and read: "You are guilty of making Five Clubs against your father."

"I object to the word 'guilty.' "

The jurors leaned forward.

"And what word would you like to replace it?"

"Thinking correctly," I offered, and then added quickly, "the way my father taught me to think."

"Thinking correctly," he repeated.

"Yes, Your Honor. As much as I loved and respected my father, I could not always accept his word as law. Parents teach their children to think. But when our thinking doesn't match theirs we are labeled upstarts, mavericks, disrespectful, and finally disobedient." (I tugged at my suit, trying to cover my navel.)

"There is some truth in what you're saying." The judge spoke in the direction of the jury. "I have nine children ranging from two to ten. My six-year-old gives me a lot of trouble; he's either high or low, depending upon his mood." They all laughed. "But I'm making him learn to think for himself."

"My father also told me to always 'face city hall' when taking a finesse. Now what am I supposed to do in the middle of Hong Kong? Stop the game and inquire which way is city hall?"

"Now don't be malapert," he cautioned.

"Bridge sayings are cute, but they will never replace logic, probabilities, percentages, or common sense."

"So you're pleading innocent?"

"There you go — labels again. Daddy taught me quite a few bridgeisms. I'm sorry they are incorrect, but look at how many people around the world are playing the same dumb things, and what's worse — they believe them."

"Such as?"

" 'Eight ever — nine never,' and how about 'The Queen always lies over the Jack.' Sounds like it should be in the Kamasutra, not bridge."

He cleared his throat and asked that my last remark be stricken from the record.

"I think we should let the hand speak for itself. And if you agree with me, then once and for all let those bridgeisms be stricken from the record."

"I think that's fair," Judge Ace said to the jury and twelve honorable Honors nodded in agreement. "Let's bring in the blackboard and view the hand," he said to the Joker. Carefully, I recorded the following hand:

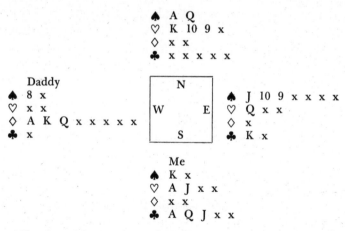

```
                        ♠  A Q
                        ♡  K 10 9 x
                        ◇  x x
                        ♣  x x x x x

        Daddy                 N
    ♠  8 x                              ♠  J 10 9 x x x x x
    ♡  x x              W        E      ♡  Q x x
    ◇  A K Q x x x x x                  ◇  x
    ♣  x                   S            ♣  K x

                        Me
                    ♠  K x
                    ♡  A J x x
                    ◇  x x
                    ♣  A Q J x x
```

All vulnerable, South (me) dealer:

Bidding:	Me	Daddy	Partner	Opponent
	1 Club	4 Diamonds	5 Clubs	Pass
	Pass	Pass		

Opening Lead: King of Diamonds

"As you can see I had two problems. Where was the Queen of Hearts and where was the King of Clubs?" I glanced in the direction of the jury: the Queen of Hearts and the King of Clubs were sitting very erect. "And after I lost the first two Diamond tricks I couldn't afford to lose any more.

"Now," I continued, "if I followed my father's sayings I would just plunk down the Ace of Clubs hoping for the King to drop, and then plop down the Jack of Hearts waiting for Daddy to cover with his Queen — who according to him would always be lying over the Jack."

The Ace of Spades interrupted. "Not before taking the safety play of laying down the Ace of Hearts first — just in case East has a singleton."

"Well, Your Honor, I didn't follow the rules laid down to me. But I did follow other rules Daddy had taught me. Rules of thinking, reasoning, logic, and to do your best at all times."

My right-hand opponent had only one Diamond, so this left Daddy with eight Diamonds, certainly enough for a vulnerable jump overcall. He really didn't have to have any other high cards. That was reasoning. After Daddy cashed the second Diamond he switched to the 8 of Spades. Now this could be a singleton, so I couldn't take a chance and cash another Spade to get a further count on his hand. I won the spade in the dummy and led a Club. The hand on my right played low, so there I was.

The jury leaned forward. The Judge leaned forward. The Joker leaned.

"What to do," I repeated, just like Perry Mason, and I leaned a little, too. "Daddy had always said the King of Clubs is alone so I . . . I thought." It was necessary to reconstruct his hand and then use the tables of percentages and probabilities to uncover the best line of play.

Daddy's four unknown cards had to be from among the still missing two Clubs, five Hearts, and six Spades (East had discarded one). Logically, there seemed a better chance they'd be Hearts and Spades, but the mathematicians have some absurd rule that this doesn't change the probabilities a priori, so I considered only the Club suit.

The three missing cards figured to divide 2–1 exactly 78 per cent of the time. One time in three, 26 per cent, the singleton would be the King. In only half of that 26 per cent would it be in the hand behind me. "So I would find Daddy holding the bare King — pardon the expression, Your Honor — only thirteen times in one hundred. At these odds, thirteen seemed like an unlucky number, so I finessed. And it worked."

"Now having pulled trumps I could go back to trying to count out Daddy's hand. Remember he had eight Diamonds, one Club, and so far one Spade. I played another Spade and he followed. If that was his last Spade, as the high-low indicated, then he had only two Hearts. Right?"

"Right," they all chimed.

Well, five missing cards of a suit figure to divide 3–2 only 68 per cent of the time, but in this case I could ignore the other 32 per cent because Daddy could not have more than two Hearts. (I believed his high-low Spade showing a doubleton.) Mentally, I dealt five cards into two piles and decided I would soon go broke if I bet that any particular card — in this case the Queen — was in the pile of two cards and not in the pile of three. Now, no matter how much the Queen always preferred lying over the Jack, as Daddy had informed me, I wasn't willing to give 3–2 odds on her getting her way *every* time. So I finessed the other way.

"And, Your Honor, the finesse worked. Apparently in such matters even a Queen's taste cannot successfully flout the Laws of Mathematics. It is difficult to undo years of conditioning, but it had to be done. Like all of us I loved my father dearly, but like all fathers he was not perfect."

The jury stayed out of the room only a few minutes. The

Judge Ace concurred with their decision to free me — innocent, they called it. And he was big enough to admit that sometimes things do have to be corrected for the good of the game. Even at the cost of defying your parents.

"And let it be known," the Ace declared, "that all misleading bridge sayings shall be null and void."

"Thank you, Your Honor."

"In Hong Kong there is no city hall." He winked at me.

His Honor led me to the drain and assured me that with a big push from him I would once again find myself in my own back-yard pool. I waved good-bye and, with his hand firmly on my rump (men will be men), he shoved me up the drain.

I surfaced happily back into the sunlight. The water and sky were just as I had left them and so was the conversation.

LIBIDO: You'll never get that chapter finished, making like Esther Williams all day.

ID: You're right. Think I'll just skip it and go on to the next one.

4—

Love and Marriage

KITCHEN, LIVING ROOM, and now the bedroom. You haven't lived until bridge moves into your king-size bed. We spent our honeymoon — where else? — at a bridge tournament. My brand-new, bridge-playing spouse was downstairs racking up another victory while I was upstairs trying on blue nightgowns, white nightgowns, green nightgowns, rejecting ones with hearts, diamonds, clubs, and spades sprinkled across the front. Finally the moment came. Tall, dark, handsome, my lifetime partner away from the table as well as at the table came thundering through the door, bridge score in hand. There I was, perfumed, coiffed, adorable —

"You'll never believe what happened to me on Hand Number Six." He waved the scorecard excitedly. "I held four Spades —"

"Just a minute," I said as calmly as possible. "It's very late and we don't have time for both. You did play twenty-eight hands, didn't you?" I stretched languidly across the bed. "One thing or another."

It took him all of five seconds. He looked at the scorecard, then me, then again at the card. "Well, on Hand Number One I held five Hearts, four Spades . . ."

Bridge players aren't any different from golfers, tennis players, fishermen, or bowlers. And just as in these sports, when a husband and wife do it together the fur starts to fly. The old, old question why?

Mine, besides being a bridger, was a tennis pro and a golf nut. We played mixed doubles together, where I learned the winning ingredients in amateur mixed doubles. Always get your first serve in; always keep the ball in play, no matter how; and develop a good net game. I managed to do all three fairly well. So how come one day when he yelled at me to lob I lobbed over the net, out of the court, and over the adjacent parking lot? I was, also, a good putter — my irons were lousy but I was really a good putter. So how come when Brown Eyes told me during a two-ball foursome to just "lay it up close" and *he'd* sink it, I putted it right off the green? Black marriage magic? I think it's mainly a matter of ego. In both cases as his inflated, mine deflated. It is essential to have a good sense of ego to be confident — not necessarily a highly inflated one, but rather one that's in its proper place. Ego is a very tricky three-letter word. Most people never deal with it. It makes you uncomfortable 'cause it's always hanging in there.

At this point in my life I was not aware of its role. What I was aware of was my ability to play bridge with other people quite successfully and to play mixed doubles really well with other women's husbands. They wouldn't have dared yell at me any more than I would have dared scoff at them.

One day I was fortunate enough to find myself on the court with visiting celebrity Don Budge. There was something going on between Mr. Budge and me that did not happen when I was playing with my husband. What was it? He was giving me confidence. He praised my attempt to do the right thing, so my lobs were deep and in the court. He acknowledged my efforts and in turn got me to play way over my head . . . not way over the parking lot. And so it was later on with an equally great bridge player, Charles Schapiro. He gave me confidence at the table. He encouraged me to think, but if I did something wrong he realized it was not done on purpose. Just inexperience — like the first chicken you burn instead of broil. These kindnesses, for want of another word, were getting good results. If from strangers, then why not from intimates. Perhaps the very same reasons that caused Lydia and Karl's conflict back when I was twelve could very easily penetrate and permeate my life. What to do about it? If the problems loomed on the horizon, the solutions were long in coming. After all, we were young and married and in love. The tennis balls and golf balls were as new and shiny as our lives.

Just like millions of other couples, eventually we fell into fun bridge with another duo. The boys had a lot to talk about and the girls were still on the natural high of young marrieds. Bridge, the game we all loved, was a great way to get together.

They oohed and aahed over our new house, the bridge table stood shiny and firm with its carefully initialed cover, the chairs all matched like little soldiers, the bar was ready for service, we had carefully sharpened pencils and new glistening tallies — it was all so comfortable and cozy as we sat down partnered with our "spice" (spouses) .

"How about a twentieth just to keep it interesting?" asked Paul.

"Sure," said my husband. The girls, of course, had nothing to say.

"Cut for deal." And away we went, innocent victims of a madness called husband-wife bridge.

"Do you play anything we should know about?" I asked.

"Nope. Just straight Mamma-Poppa bridge."

That sounded so cute. After all, they had only been married a few months. Before we knew what happened Poppa Paul had bid a Heart, Mamma Minnie had bid three Hearts, and the bidding went pass, pass!, pass. Poor dear Minnie, I thought, imagine getting passed in a forcing situation. They went down one trick. I offered them a drink as Hubby said to me, "How many Spades did you have?"

"Four."

"I see," he replied.

And from the bar, "I don't see."

"You will."

Translated, this all means: Poppa Paul psyched* a Heart, trusting Minnie raised to three, and we were cold for 4 Spades. Some way to start a lifetime (?) foursome at the table much less a lifetime (??) twosome away from it.

"Paul's so cute," said Minnie. "He's always playing tricks on me and keeping me off balance." I made a mental note never to buy a car from him.

Next deal my husband opened the bidding with 1 Notrump. We were playing a new (at the time) system called Texas Transfer. As the responder, if you wanted the hand to be played from the opening bidder's side of the table in your suit, you would respond one under the final contract. There have been subsequent changes in the system, but originally it went like this:

Opener		Responder
1 NT	or	4 Diamonds = partner should bid 4 Hearts
1 NT		4 Hearts = partner should bid 4 Spades

Naturally the responder's hand must justify the bid
in suit length and count.

I responded 4 Diamonds, thrilled I had remembered the new

---

* A bid intended to interfere with the opponents' bidding and play; not to aid the bidding or play of one's own side.

system *he* had just taught me. He glared. He puffed away. He looked at the ceiling. Aloud: "There's no such bid as Four Diamonds." He shrugged, looked at Paul, who was in complete sympathy, and bid "Five Diamonds." Crestfallen, I bid 5 Hearts. Down one.

Then and there I learned never to crack your partner over the knuckles for a mistake he hates himself (as much as you do) for making. Never. I think today Hubby might apologize (not necessary but nice), but that night he said we would drop Texas from our bidding jargon. Paul and Minnie immediately added it to theirs. It is a good system and I recommend it to partnerships.

We played a few rubbers and then switched partners, just for fun. Mate-swapping wasn't the vogue in those days, but in some remote way this was its fourth cousin once-removed. Charming, adorable Paul smiling at me as I fluffed 6 Hearts, refilling my glass as I doubled and they made it. My husband, who scowled at me for putting him in an unmakable game, telling Minnie as they went down six: "It was all on a finesse."

I want to play with my husband, dammit, and I'm going to make it work, were my thoughts as I put the bridge table away for the night — shiny and new? It looked like a scarred battlefield! And those matched chairs were indeed soldiers. Only now their legs were in need of bandages. I climbed the stairs, anxious to see how the night of married bridge at home had affected my husband. I hoped he wasn't agonizing over the Texas misbid. He wasn't. The only state he was in was one of deep sleep.

I fell asleep knowing that bridge wasn't exactly the best thing for your sex life. Maybe we should take up strip poker. No, Minnie's too cute for that. On the other hand, Paul . . . Snzzzz.

The following week we went to Paul and Minnie's. Same set as our house, only Minnie and Paul had thought up a new gimmick. "Let's put all of the money won into a kitty, and when we have enough for dinner we'll go someplace nice — maybe even dance." Oh, the whole thing was so young and romantic and married.

"But," I offered, "let's try to keep the bridge serious." This seems to be one of the pitfalls of couple bridge. Not that you have to play every card as if it were a matter of life and death, but you can't be serious one minute and joking the next. Or serious until you make a mistake and then laugh it off. If you play for an eightieth to keep it interesting, well, then keep it interesting.

My husband and I got into a very complicated series of bids. Complicated for me at that point in my bridge life, but basic.

Husband	Me
1 Heart	3 Hearts
4 NT*	5 Diamonds
6 Clubs	???

We had agreed on Hearts as the trump suit, 4 Notrump was Blackwood, but the 6 Club bid was new. Six Hearts was available for me to bid, but in my head all kinds of strange reactions were taking place. What did 6 Clubs mean?

1. He's making a smart-ass bid.
2. He psyched the Heart suit and is trying to land in his suit of Clubs.
3. We are off two Club tricks so he's trying to prevent the lead and still play 6 Hearts.
4. Why is he making life so complicated for me?
Then I turned my head around!

Answers to:

1. He's a good player, so discard this.
2. Just because he's psyched before, why do you have to think that's what he is doing now. Discard this.

* Blackwood.

3. Maybe he might pull this going to 3 Notrump, but he's on your side and *he* could have bid 6 Hearts. Discard this.

4. He is not doing this to you. This is a new situation!

Earlier that day I had been reading a speech by Dr. William Osler that he had made to a graduating class at Harvard Medical School. One of his points to the up-and-coming doctors was: "Always listen to your patients; they are trying to tell you something." I looked at my husband; he was trying to tell me something and I had to discard all of the above thoughts — thoughts that came to me out of my ignorance of the bid, cover-up thoughts. What is he trying to tell me? Through a series of reasoning I finally figured out he was worried about the quality of the trump suit.

1. After I responded 5 Diamonds he could have quit at 5 Hearts, so we must have all four Aces.

2. In order to check for Aces via Blackwood he had lost the bid of 5 Notrump, the usual Grand Slam Force. Because now 5 Notrump would ask for Kings.

3. He did not go right to 6 Hearts so what was he asking? The 6 Club bid was a substitute for the Grand Slam Force: "Partner, bid 7 Hearts if you hold two of the top three Heart honors."

Listen to your partner; he is trying to tell you something. I see husband-wife bridge as instant partnership development. If Hubby psyched on a previous hand you must trust him on the next. If Hubby fails to show for dinner won't you still be in the kitchen the next night? And the night after?

A great big smile crossed my face as I bid 7 Hearts and he made it. I had found one key to the locked chamber of married bridge: Listen. This had a good effect on him, too. Maybe he wasn't aware of what had happened — God knows, he couldn't get inside my head — but he knew something had happened. And if it worked once it would work again. I mentally noted it in my "how to get along with husband" book: Listen to your partner.

Our bridge togetherness against Minnie and Paul began to take a different turn. They started with labels: "You're so lucky," "You always hold great cards," "Our finesses never work," "You always find the lucky opening lead." And then, finally, "Pat, you take this game too seriously!"

Their remedy was to add two more couples. Now we were a matched set of eight. And Sunday nights were designated as couple card night. We rotated houses, all pitched in with the food, and someone always had to bring an extra table. We started off playing set games, which means husbands and wives as regular partners. And again the money would go into the pot. This time for our big New Year's Eve party together.

We cut the cards for the first round and drew Maxine and Lester. They were the old married pair — they had eight months of togetherness on us. Lester had no problem on the first hand. "One Notrump," he sneered from the left side of his mouth as the right side bit harder on his pipe. Maxine popped him right into game, 3 Notrump, and off we went. Correction, off they went — down one.

> MAXINE: How many points did you have?
> LESTER: Enough to bid Notrump.
> MAXINE: How many Hearts did you have?
> LESTER: I don't remember!
> MAXINE: Well, it seems to me —
> LESTER: What seems to you —

And on and on they went through the pipe tapping, through the peanuts I noticed Maxine would dip into after each sentence, and through the night.

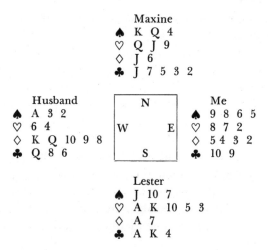

Maxine
♠ K Q 4
♡ Q J 9
♢ J 6
♣ J 7 5 3 2

Husband
♠ A 3 2
♡ 6 4
♢ K Q 10 9 8
♣ Q 8 6

Me
♠ 9 8 6 5
♡ 8 7 2
♢ 5 4 3 2
♣ 10 9

Lester
♠ J 10 7
♡ A K 10 5 3
♢ A 7
♣ A K 4

Opening Lead: Diamond King

Let's examine what went wrong and why. Lester opened the bidding incorrectly. He has a fine five-card major suit, so why conceal it? I wonder if Notrump and "I'm the head of the house" are synonymous? "I pay all the bills so I'll play all the Notrumps." Okay, for the moment we'll accept that, but only for the moment. Next, he found himself in this impossible contract with the knowledge that 4 Hearts is cold. Now what? His ego pushed him into this bid and now his ego will push him into the incorrect line of play. If he ran the Heart suit Maxine would spot five Hearts immediately. No good. Maybe the Club Queen would fall? Unlikely. But maybe he could sneak a Spade through? And this would be the real ego builder because it would make the opponents look sleepy. Lester ducked the opening lead, winning the Diamond return perforce. He played a low Spade toward the dummy. If this went through he would have five Hearts, one Diamond, two Clubs, and one Spade — making 3 Notrump. But my partner was wide awake and stepped up with the Ace of Spades, then cashed three Diamonds for a total of five tricks, or down one.

And then Lester and Maxine went at it. She knew that Lester knew that she knew he had five Hearts. What did she have to gain by bringing it up? What she could gain was a chance to improve her game. By telling her ego to shut up and not regale Lester with her verbal abuse she could turn her attention to how to make the hand. And that's instant improvement.

After the second Diamond lead is won with the Ace, quietly take stock. Maybe by running the five Hearts West will run into difficulty. It's certainly worth the chance. Maybe not as showy as trying to slip the Spade through, but the object of the game is to make the game. By the time the fourth Heart is cashed West is immobilized.

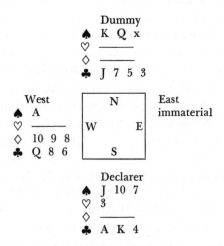

```
                        Dummy
                     ♠ K Q x
                     ♡ ——————
                     ◊ ——————
                     ♣ J 7 5 3

        West              N           East
     ♠ A                              immaterial
     ♡ ——————    W           E
     ◊ 10 9 8
     ♣ Q 8 6              S

                       Declarer
                     ♠ J 10 7
                     ♡ 3
                     ◊ ——————
                     ♣ A K 4
```

If West discards a Club your Jack will produce the ninth trick; if a Diamond is discarded then you can safely play a Spade — making 3 Notrump and making it as a good partner.

And if you've really got it together you don't need to tell anyone that you could have made the hand.

5—

What Are You Doing New Year's Eve?

PLAYING BRIDGE? The matched set of eight gathered at eight. A little bridge, a little champagne, a little kissing, and a lot of bypassing four-card major suit fits. We were eight just like the magic number in bridge. Seventy-five per cent of the time when you hold, in the combined hands, eight cards of either major suit, that's where your trump spot oughta be. Just like you knew your future spot when your dream guy appeared with red hair and freckles, that's where you oughta be and that's where you are. Eight Hearts or 8 Spades — that's your future spot.

If your partner opens the bidding with a Club or a Diamond and you have enough points to respond, why do you think 1 Notrump is weaker than 1 Spade or 1 Heart? 'Tis not true. Today, when so many players open only five-card majors, it is imperative to show your four-card major when responding. For if you fail to do so, your partner will never believe you have one.

Paul, Minnie, Lester, and Maxine started in one room and we sat down opposite Joshua and Jenny, numbers seven and eight of our octagonal set. They bought the first hand for — guess what? — 3 Notrump. Wanna guess who was playing it? Right.

Joshua. For the moment just examine the bidding and the first three cards played. Circles denote cards already played.

Bidding:
	Jenny	Joshua	
	1 Diamond	1 Notrump	(no bidding inter-
	2 Notrump	3 Notrump	ference from us)

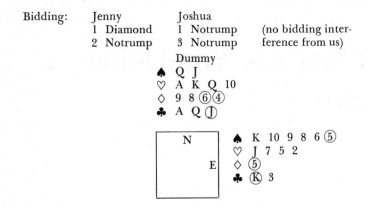

```
                        Dummy
                   ♠  Q  J
                   ♡  A  K  Q  10
                   ◊  9  8 ⑥④
                   ♣  A  Q ①
       ┌──────────────┐
       │  N           │   ♠  K  10  9  8  6 ⑤
       │              │   ♡  J  7  5  2
       │          E   │   ◊ ⑤
       │              │   ♣ Ⓚ 3
       └──────────────┘
```

My husband led the King of Diamonds, which Joshua ducked. Hubby continued with the Queen; I discarded a low Spade; Joshua won it with the Ace from his hand. He then led a low Club to the dummy, finessing the Jack, which I won with the King. I'll give you all the information I had so you can make the next play before I disclose the entire hand.

Joshua waved his cards around as if to say "That's all," but he did not make a direct claim — only because his other hand had reached for his glass of champagne. If you ever make a claim, remember, you must tell the opponents exactly how you intend to play the hand, with no finesses, and accounting for all outstanding trumps. The penalties are heavy if you fail to do so. Now sometimes a player will make a premature claim from inexperience or lack of knowledge. You have the right to challenge and play the rest of the hand out with the declarer's cards exposed. I just told Joshua to enjoy his drink because I wanted to think about the hand. And to think about him.

Having somewhat mastered the technique of listening to partner's voice, now turn your attention to the opponents' voices and acquire additional helpful hints. I began to wonder if Joshua had concealed a four-card Heart suit to make certain he would play Notrump. If you are solving this problem along with me in the construction of his hand, let's assume he's guilty. And that maybe he has a long Club suit — after all, his first play was a Club. So his Spade suit must be short. And if it's the Ace and one other card, he can be prevented from ever reaching his hand again. However, if he holds the Jack of Hearts and the Spade Ace, then his halfhearted claim would be valid. But he didn't, so always take a crack at setting a hand; don't concede unless declarer lays it out.

I switched to the King of Spades — didn't you?

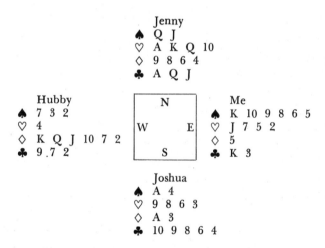

```
                        Jenny
                      ♠ Q J
                      ♡ A K Q 10
                      ◇ 9 8 6 4
                      ♣ A Q J
     Hubby              ┌─────────┐        Me
   ♠ 7 3 2              │    N    │      ♠ K 10 9 8 6 5
   ♡ 4                  │ W     E │      ♡ J 7 5 2
   ◇ K Q J 10 7 2       │         │      ◇ 5
   ♣ 9 . 7 2            │    S    │      ♣ K 3
                        └─────────┘
                        Joshua
                      ♠ A 4
                      ♡ 9 8 6 3
                      ◇ A 3
                      ♣ 10 9 8 6 4
```

As you can see 4 Hearts, not 3 Notrump, is a shooin. Joshua did not lead his partner and himself to the Promised Land as promised.

"Well, Jenny," he said, "it was all on the Club finesse." Famous last words — words I hope you don't find yourself saying over and over because you are once again in the wrong contract.

As notorious as men are for hogging Notrump contracts,

women are just as adept at sidestepping them. None of us came into the world afraid of playing them, so how come? Conditioning, maybe? Today many teachers start beginners with only the play of Notrump to circumvent this unfounded fear.

Around midnight Joshua had finished his sixth hand in Notrump as well as his sixth glass of champagne. A very dismayed Minnie appeared with a new remedy for the New Year.

"Let's split up into the girls versus the boys." The boys thought it was a ripping good thought and I wondered if they would ever play any contracts other than Notrump! I mentally heard an auction like this:

My husband	Paul	Joshua	Lester
1 Notrump	2 Notrump	3 Notrump	4 Notrump
5 Notrump	6 Notrump	7 Notrump	8 Notrump!

So the boys, armed with more champagne, took their seats and the girls, unarmed, cut to see how we'd split up. Minnie and I against Lester and Joshua. What a way to start the New Year — 1951. And right away I was tested and almost failed.

Minnie opened the bidding with 1 Diamond and I held *that* four-card major I've been harping about. And I'm afraid some of the male thoughts were harbored in my mind. To myself: This hand probably belongs in Notrump. I can play it better than Minnie. Maybe she doesn't have a fit with me. If I bid my suit then she'll bid Notrump! She'll blow it. I hate myself — I really do.

More to myself: This is exactly how Paul thinks. And Lester, Joshua, and my own dearly beloved. Now I'm playing Head of the House. How do I feel when I am treated like this? Lousy. Minnie is my friend and you don't do bad things to your friend. You build where you can.

"Aren't you going to bid?" Minnie asked after Joshua had passed.

"One Heart," I responded with all my heart. There it was. (Ego, you stay home with the cat.) And if you don't give your partner that vote of confidence you aren't going to have a good partner.

"Pass," grumbled Lester.

"One Notrump" by Minnie, hardly believing her words.

I bid 3 Notrump and Minnie delivered the goods. There were no audible words between us but a million silent ones in our shared looks.

"Just lucky," one of the spice uttered.

Minnie must have remembered saying just that to us one evening as she replied, "I've never met anyone who liked being called unlucky."

The next hand was almost a repeat of the first and again she was playing 3 Notrump. For Minnie's sake and the good of my soul, here is her play of the hand.

```
                        Me
                     ♠ 7 4
                     ♡ Q 7 4
                     ◇ A 4 2
                     ♣ A K Q 9 2

      Lester              N              Joshua
   ♠ K 10                              ♠ Q 9 8 5
   ♡ J 9 8 6 3      W         E        ♡ K 10 2
   ◇ J 10 8 5                          ◇ 9 6
   ♣ 6 3                 S             ♣ J 10 8 7

                      Minnie
                     ♠ A J 6 3 2
                     ♡ A 5
                     ◇ K Q 7 3
                     ♣ 5 4
```

Bidding:

	North (Me)	East (Joshua)	South (Minnie)	West (Lester)
	1 Club	Pass	1 Spade	Pass
	2 Clubs	Pass	3 Notrump	Pass
	Pass	Pass		

Opening Lead: Heart 6

Minnie pondered the opening lead for quite a while. She was right — she didn't want to make the guess of the Heart King at trick one. Correctly, she ducked in the dummy and won East's 10 with the Ace in her hand. Off the top she had three Club tricks, three Diamond tricks, one Heart, and one Spade for a total of 8. If needed, she could always play for the King of Hearts to be onside, so for the moment she postponed her decision and attacked the Club suit. She led the 5 from her hand and when Lester played low Minnie played the 9 from the dummy. I don't ever remember her making such an astute maneuver at the table, and I think it is safe to say I was as pleased as she. East won the 9 and was helpless. Now the Club suit could produce the ninth trick. If East makes the desperate move of playing a Heart, Minnie will have an overtrick. In this case it was definitely "Do put off 'til it matters what hasn't to be done right away."

Paul, husband of Minnie, sauntered into our room to inquire how we were getting along. Lester was quick to tell him how lucky we were as we had wrapped up the first rubber. Minnie looked up and said to Paul, "We're doing just fine, but I do miss you." Then and there I knew Minnie would always be okay.

We started the final rubber of the New Year, generally known as "the return." The boys were anxious to get even or to prove it was just luck — or maybe to get in a few Notrump licks of their own. Minnie and I traded seats as a gesture to improve their luck! But the Gods moved with us and I was the declarer on the next hand.

Minnie was funny when she bid 1 Notrump. Both boys looked at her as though she had swallowed Notrump pills, but I believed her and that's the name of the game. I played the King of Spades from the dummy; Joshua won with the Ace and returned the Jack. My first impulse was to discard on dummy's good Queen, but my second impulse was better. Wait. Minnie had postponed

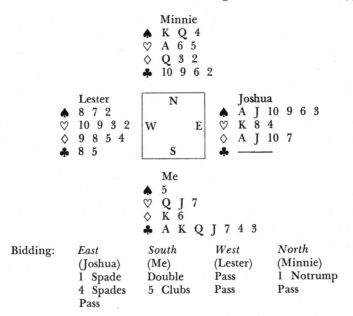

Minnie
♠ K Q 4
♡ A 6 5
♢ Q 3 2
♣ 10 9 6 2

Lester
♠ 8 7 2
♡ 10 9 3 2
♢ 9 8 5 4
♣ 8 5

Joshua
♠ A J 10 9 6 3
♡ K 8 4
♢ A J 10 7
♣ ——————

Me
♠ 5
♡ Q J 7
♢ K 6
♣ A K Q J 7 4 3

Bidding:	East	South	West	North
	(Joshua)	(Me)	(Lester)	(Minnie)
	1 Spade	Double	Pass	1 Notrump
	4 Spades	5 Clubs	Pass	Pass
	Pass			

Opening Lead: 8 of Spades

her decision in the previous hand, and her play set my thinking cap on straight. (Isn't it a beautiful partnership game on all levels?) I wasn't sure which discard to make. The discard of a Heart looked good, but if the finesse failed I still had to lose the Diamond Ace, which totaled down one — and a lousy way to start the New Year. So I trumped it, postponing the discard decision. I played the Club Ace followed by a low Club to dummy's 9. This was followed by a low Diamond from the dummy; and then East had the problem. If he hopped up with the Ace he would not get a Heart trick. I could then discard one Heart on the good Spade and the other on the Queen of Diamonds. If he played low, then the King of Diamonds would win the trick and the losing Diamond would go on the Spade Queen. Making five.

It was all so much fun. Married, in love, champagne, New

Year's Eve, and what a great game bridge really is. Wow! And a cementing of the friendship with Minnie on a new level. I'll always remember her on another hand, which was the very last one we played against them, Paul and Minnie, as a couple prior to my subsequent departure from Baltimore. Every time it was Paul's turn to bid, he bid Hearts. Minnie passed with equal deliberation. Hubby and I were bidding Spades just as rambunctiously as Paul was bidding Hearts. Finally we bought the hand for 4 Spades, but only after Paul had bid up to 4 Hearts by himself. Minnie led the Ace of Hearts. Paul stared transfixedly at the card and exploded, *"I didn't know you had that card!"* Minnie smiled. "You bid it so many times I thought you had it." Suffice it to say, their humor sustained them at the table — and I'm sure away from it, too.

When the magic eight met the first Sunday in the New Year, it was Maxine who suggested the girls play together and let the boys play as a foursome. This was especially appealing to me, as only that afternoon on the tennis court my husband had asked me to please just cover the alley when at net. He would cover the rest of the court! Humiliating? Right. But when the ball came toward me and he told me to duck — that did it. I walked off the court for good. Whatever I was learning about ego and the like at the bridge table I couldn't put to use elsewhere. So when Maxine made her suggestion I seconded it pretty quickly.

I was wondering if eventually the girls would play in one house and the boys in another, but it never quite came to that. What it did come to was my husband's forming an all-men's game once a week at our house. I stayed around long enough to serve the pretzels and Scotch and then would take off to play duplicate. I had met Irv Fisher at my husband's regular game, and it was only natural that he would introduce me to his partner, Charles Schapiro. And so it was that between the two of them I always managed to have a good partner/teacher for my once-a-week outings. One evening while playing duplicate, Charles and I found ourselves playing against Maxine and Lester. As we arranged the cards, I hastily explained Maxine and Lester to Charles along with the evolution of the magic eight and the birth of my husband's "for men only" night. Charles was quick to point out that playing against the same people time after time was a distinct advantage. As I mulled this over in my mind the bidding went as follows:

Bidding:	*North*	*East*	*South*	*West*
	(Charles)	(Maxine)	(Me)	(Lester)
	1 Club	Pass	2 Notrump	Pass
	3 Notrump	Pass	Pass	Pass

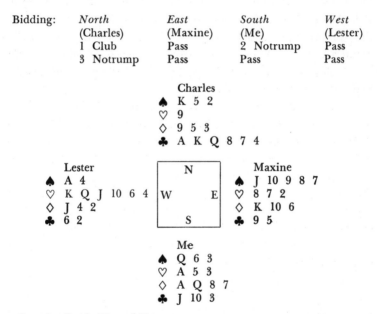

```
                      Charles
                    ♠ K 5 2
                    ♡ 9
                    ◇ 9 5 3
                    ♣ A K Q 8 7 4

     Lester            ┌─────────┐        Maxine
   ♠ A 4               │    N    │      ♠ J 10 9 8 7
   ♡ K Q J 10 6 4      │ W     E │      ♡ 8 7 2
   ◇ J 4 2             │         │      ◇ K 10 6
   ♣ 6 2               │    S    │      ♣ 9 5
                       └─────────┘
                      Me
                    ♠ Q 6 3
                    ♡ A 5 3
                    ◇ A Q 8 7
                    ♣ J 10 3
```

Opening Lead: King of Hearts

The total tricks on this hand were a quick eight. My, how that number follows one about! I ducked the Heart King and the continuation of the Queen, but was forced to win the Jack. That left Lester with three good Hearts. If he held the Ace of Spades or the King of Diamonds I was down for sure. So I decided to cash the good Clubs and see. Lester's first discard was the 4 of Spades, announcing to the trusting Maxine that he had nothing in that suit. His next two discards were the 4–2 of Diamonds, announcing the King, his entry to run the remaining Hearts. Mine sank. But rose again as the ninth trick would be a Spade after Maxine took her Ace. If she really had it. But then Charles's words flipped across my mind: "Distinct advantage playing against the same players." Now what would Lester do in this defensive situation? Didn't he continually lie to Maxine? Would it upset her applecart on this hand if he continued to lie? But it could upset me and it almost did. I went with the odds. Lester's not telling the truth and the fifty-fifty chance that the King of Diamonds would be onside. The reasoning worked and so did the finesse.

After they left the table Charlie congratulated me on making the hand and I thanked him for his help. However, Lester is not to be dismissed lightly on his defense. He made an all-out effort to deceive, and deception is part of the game. When you find yourself in this situation, employ the same helpful hints given to you previously by the opponents. If you know their habits, use them. But if you are the one about to make the deceptive play and the declarer is your best friend, maybe you should go with the usual — at least mix it up against people who know your game. Keep them off balance.

A game with Charlie Schapiro was always good for as many lessons as there were hands. He was playing 3 Notrump. The hand is immaterial except for the Club suit.

Dummy
K 10 9 8 7 6

Charles
A 3 2

He needed to bring in the suit to make the contract, which

means he could not afford to lose a trick or the opponents would run their long suit. Certainly you've been in this spot, and your heart beats a little faster as you make your play and look longingly at your opponents to drop the cards you need. It's the kind of nervous play made before you think you're about to give away the pack at canasta. Charlie laid down the Ace of Clubs, West followed with the 4 and East with the Queen. If you don't have prior information from the bidding or you're not playing against a Lester, you must rely on your bridge know-how. Charlie quietly noted the drop of the Queen on his right, and when he continued the suit he finessed for the Jack, just giving a cursory glance to East's card, a small Diamond. And as if it were his due, he then ran the suit. I, on the other hand, was amazed at his cool.

"I like your style, Charlie," was about as profound as I could be. "Help me to understand your play, please."

"It's called restricted choice," he replied. And then he launched into one of the lengthiest discussions I had ever heard at the table.

The Official Encyclopedia of Bridge defines it as follows: "The play of a card which may have been selected as a choice of equal plays increases the chance that the player started with a holding in which his choice was restricted." In other words, if East started with the singleton Queen, his choice was restricted to the play of it because that was his only choice!

"Now," continued Charlie, "the odds favoring the finesse as opposed to the drop are slightly less than two to one."

There are so many things to learn about bridge and so much of your mental energy is consumed by just the play of the game that I feel certain things should be accepted, not questioned. So I accepted this as law and saved myself hours of nervousness at the table wondering when to finesse and when not to. As I've already stated, if you have additional information, then use it first. But if not, accept the restricted choice play as it is backed up with correct odds, probabilities, etc. I also accepted the fact that the 4-4 major fit is supreme and saved tons of energy trying to decide whether Notrump sometimes was a better spot than a major suit.

This does not preclude tournament play, where Notrump score counts more and players are always looking for the optimum spot. But the judgment required to know exactly when Notrump is just as good and just as safe as Hearts or Spades takes years to develop. At home it is not necessary, so play the 4-4 fit. Save your energy for the countless problems that continue to arise. Making the best opening lead, the beautifully timed defensive switch, the thrill of handling the dummy correctly . . . these are the winning plays, not whether Notrump can be made as well as a major suit game.

6—

Blue Ribbon Baby

WHAT IS A National Tournament? It's where you go to have a baby. A baby that was probably conceived somewhere between 3 Notrump and 7 Hearts — game and grand slam.

It was hot and humid and miserable, so to pass the time my husband suggested we take a short forty-mile ride to Washington, D.C., to see what a National Bridge Tournament was all about. After all, if the baby decided to make an appearance, certainly the nation's capital could handle it.

We walked into the Mayflower Hotel as innocent as John and Jane Doe checking into Watergate. Hundreds of people were milling around, talking about bridge. The ten-day tournament was in its seventh day and the players reflected it. Their skin had a prison-type pallor, their clothes were rumpled, pencils that had started out six inches long were chewed down to three inches, and when I heard one man ask another how he did the night before and he replied, "You ought to know, I was your partner!" I thought we should turn around and go home.

The lobby was an array of desks, each labeled with its function: Partnerships, Sightseeing, Information, Trophies, Registration, Books and Related Bridge Items, and Scheduled Events. I sauntered over to the Partnership desk to see how it worked. There were small white cards to be filled out by the person needing a partner for a specific event: Mixed Pairs, Women's Pairs, Men's Pairs, Open Pairs, Team of Four (Mixed and Open) — it reminded me of a tennis tournament. But it was the last line on the card that told it all: How many Master Points? It's like filling out your age. To lie or not to lie? And if you lied could your prospective partner check it out? The answer to the latter is no. But the former, well . . . I watched people filling out the cards, and in each case the first part was done rapidly, but when the last line appeared each one paused. Master Points were quickly replacing blue chip stocks as status.

The parent organization of bridge, the American Contract Bridge League, awards points on a sliding scale to the winners and runners-up of all duplicate tournaments. The goal of each player is to become a Life Master, which says you have won 300 points. A certain number of these points must be won at national or regional events. They are known as red points; all others are black points. It is not uncommon for a player to amass hundreds of black points while the red ones remain elusive. As the caliber of play at national and regional events improves, it becomes more and more difficult to win those little red devils and wear the badge of Life Master.

So each player in search of a partner was lying a little on the card about his points. Sooner or later all is revealed at the table, so why not in front? Ego? And as they filled out the cards I wondered: If you're so good then how come you don't have a partner?

My husband was lost somewhere, so to pass time I mentally fondled the trophies. There was a huge one dead center nestled in black velvet, and through the glass I could see inscribed in the silver the names of famous players who had been winners, the Hank Aarons and Arnie Palmers of the bridge world. The man behind the counter gave me a warm smile and asked if the baby was a bridge player. At the moment it felt more like Lou "The Toe" Groza of the football world.

"We're entered in the Novice Pairs this afternoon." My husband came winging across the floor, waving the entry form at me. Novice, because we had fewer than 50 Master Points.

"Do you think it's fair? After all, we'll be three against two." A gentle reminder.

"It'll be good for you, for me, for him. Okay?"

"I guess so." And with that we found our section, table, opponents, and off we went into the world of high-level tournament bridge. All three of us.

We played pretty well for the next four hours, and it did take my mind off my excessive size. When we finished I did the normal thing — got ready to go home.

"Let's hang around for the scores," he suggested. That seemed reasonable so we did, and when it was all tabulated we were first. Again, thinking we were finished, I got ready to go home. And then the bomb fell.

"What do you mean we can't leave? What do you mean it's a three-session event? What's three sessions?"

"Well, Pat, there are single-session events, double-session, and we are in a three-session one." All national championships are at least three sessions. By that time the men are supposed to be separated from the boys. In other words, you can play single-session events (four hours) and pick up a black point if you're lucky, but the big titles are settled over a longer period of time, which is certainly fair. But I was having my own main event, played over nine continuous monthly sessions.

"So," he continued, "we'll have dinner and play the second session." And that's exactly what we did. When the second session was scored we were still in first place. Now the excitement began to take over. All the way back to Baltimore we chatted happily about the hands, couldn't believe we were really leading the field, so close in our first attempt — we even forgot to fight. But we still had to face the next day, and when it arrived I felt lousy. Strange pains and rumblings were going on.

"I don't think we should go. We'll just have to explain and say we're sorry." My husband's face fell as flat as an overcooked soufflé. It reminded me of my face the night of our honeymoon. I had lost that round and I was about to lose this one. According to the officials, you cannot drop out of an event unless you die. And this seems to be the attitude of the addicts as well. One lady tripped as she walked into the bridge room, played the afternoon session, and then had her broken ankle attended to. During a tournament on Long Island a fire broke out, and one player refused to evacuate the hotel until he had finished a slam hand that would guarantee his victory. So if Baryshnikov can dance with a broken ankle, why not a bridge player? And I guess that's what I was doing en route to Washington with the intermittent pains. We took our places at the table and were recognized for the first time. My husband thought it was because we were leading the field; I thought it was because of my size.

"When do you expect your baby?" the first pair asked.

"Any minute."

"Guess we'd better hurry," they laughed. And in their hurry dropped 24 out of a possible 28 points into our laps.

Next table: "So you're the pair leading the field. Can't miss you, ha-ha." He was being so cute he forgot to count trumps and dropped another 20 points. Ha-ha.

We were both learning a good lesson about competition. No matter what the circumstances, if you're in it then keep your mind on what you're doing. There is practically no margin for error at the table. Every deuce counts, and your mind better be on the cards. In tournaments the element of luck depends mainly on what hands you play against good players and what hands you play against bad players. After three sessions or more this figures to balance out. Whether you have good or bad cards really doesn't matter because your opponents are playing the same hands. Once the cards are dealt, they are placed in small slotted boards. The boards are passed from table to table until each team has had a crack at them. By playing the same hands you can compare your score to everyone else's. Unlike rubber bridge where you shuffle and redeal after every hand.

Most of the final session we were defending while our opponents were playing the hands. It is very discouraging to defend twenty-four hands out of twenty-eight. You never get the feeling that you're in the game. But if you are defending most hands, then so are the other players sitting in your direction. So outdefend them.

On round five I was sitting East and had to make an important opening lead. As I pulled a card the baby kicked, and the card fell out of my hand face down on the floor. Did the baby know something I didn't know? I changed my mind and the lead. The new lead set the hand.

"That's some baby," the opponent remarked, looking at *us* with instant hate. "I may learn to dislike babies!"

Halfway through the session I went out into the lobby to find my new and only friend, the man behind the trophy counter. (I did not consider my husband my friend at the moment. He was estimating our score, making notes, and puffing frantically on a premature cigar, which made me ill.)

Mr. Cohen was dusting off the trophies. He asked how we were doing and was quite controlled until I asked him if he knew a doctor. "You're kidding, of course?"

"Not exactly. Every time a round is called [at fifteen-minute intervals] I get a pain."

I remember his exact words: "Oh, my God." He wiped his brow with the dustcloth.

"Mr. Cohen, I have only five minutes before I return to the table. Please think. You're the only person I know here and I can't upset my partner."

"Why not?"

" 'Cause he'll play badly." In retrospect that was inaccurate. He never even heard me when I told him I had consulted a doctor, who thought I was in labor. I managed to find a doctor/player who between hands asked me what type of Notrumps we played, how we were doing, and, yes, the description of my pains sounded good to him. And as he scurried back to his table, as an afterthought he told me to find him if the pains increased to five-minute intervals.

It's amazing how people never listen. The next round, a kind old lady asked how I felt. I told her I was in labor and she said, "That's nice. Bid."

What was I doing in this labyrinth of bridge nuts? Was Gertrude Ederle pregnant when she swam the English Channel? Did Patty Berg sink her final putt and then rush to the delivery room? What kind of commitment do all of us make to sports, games? Maybe one of the troubles is we forget they're just sports. When husband and wife are rolling up their sleeves for a battle, maybe they forget what type of activity they are about to fight over. Perspective, perspective and the wisdom to know the difference. The Chinese have a philosophy that I have tried for many years to follow. If something is disturbing you, allocate a certain length of time on which to dwell on it. Dwell on it as hard as you want, fuss about it, scream, yell — whatever your thing is — but when the time is up, that's it. Now put these two things together. First decide if what you are about to fight over is worth it, and then set a time limit. Especially in bridge. Unlike tennis, you can't take a hard swat at the ball to relieve tension. All you can do is walk to the restroom and back. Even in golf you can let out a bit of energy from shot to shot, but at the bridge table most people take shots at their partners.

I looked around the room, then at my husband, and knew this was going to be my sports arena for the next umpteen years. I was here, the baby was imminent, and only one hand to go. It was either get up and leave or give it my all. Foolishly, I tried holding my breath, thinking this would deter the child. The opponents thought I was sending out signals. Someone up there knew I'd be out of action for a while and dealt me the following blockbuster:

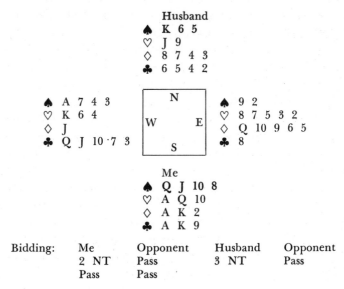

Husband
♠ K 6 5
♡ J 9
◇ 8 7 4 3
♣ 6 5 4 2

♠ A 7 4 3
♡ K 6 4
◇ J
♣ Q J 10 7 3

♠ 9 2
♡ 8 7 5 3 2
◇ Q 10 9 6 5
♣ 8

Me
♠ Q J 10 8
♡ A Q 10
◇ A K 2
♣ A K 9

Bidding:	Me	Opponent	Husband	Opponent
	2 NT	Pass	3 NT	Pass
	Pass	Pass		

Opening Lead: Club Queen

I could see eight top tricks after the Spade Ace was eliminated. The danger to the hand was if West held the Spade Ace and the King of Hearts plus the long Clubs. I won the Club Queen with the Ace and played a Spade. West won the Ace and returned another Club, which his partner failed to follow. It was time to take stock, but it was difficult. Each time West led a Club, *pow* went junior. He didn't like the leads either. My mind kept wandering . . . how am I going to make a graceful exit? Where *is* the nearest exit? I looked to the right: no exit sign. But over West's head, on my left, was an exit sign. And West was going to be my exit at the table. If you want to force an opponent to lead to you, make certain you have an exit card. And eventually I did want West to lead to me. I wasn't about to finesse a Heart. Surely he held the 10 of Clubs for his leads of the Queen-Jack. And the 9 in my hand was my exit card! I ran the Spades, cashed the Ace and King of Diamonds, and played the 9 of Clubs. West had followed to four Spades, one Diamond, was known to have five Clubs, so what difference how many Hearts? He was end-played by the exit card. He could cash his high Clubs, but was forced to play a Heart into my Ace-Queen.

I mumbled something to my husband about how he should stay and check the scores, just in case we won, and I would leave a message with Mr. Keeper of the Trophies Nat Cohen saying where I was and what I was doing.

By the time I reached the hospital the pains had stopped. "But," cautioned the doctor, "the baby was ready." I raced back to the hotel to a beaming husband. We had won! Our first National Tournament and 30 of those elusive red points. Mr. Cohen reached into the trophy case and handed me the big silver one I had been mentally fondling just twenty-eight hours before. The engraved names stood out big as life, and we were so proud to add ours to the President's Cup along with George Rapee, Eric Murray, and many others.

The trophy was two inches longer than the baby, but the baby outweighed the cup by two pounds.

7—

The Human Element

Now that I had amassed 30 red points plus a national title, I was certain the boys would ask me into their game. Nothing was farther from their minds. The nursery was the place for any new mother while Poppa played with the boys in their regular Wednesday night game. Our duplicate activity was temporarily inactive, so I had to content myself with the strains of 2 Hearts, 5 Clubs . . . familiar sounds drifting from the downstairs to the upstairs. Most of the sounds were pleasant until one night — *bam*.

"You looked in my hand," yelled one man. "You could never have dropped that King unless you looked."

I covered the baby's ears — hardly the sounds a newborn should hear.

"He probably played with Pat's father," I heard my husband say. "He always dropped singleton Kings." My husband was trying to fluff it off.

"How dare you say that to me," the second voice screamed. "You're accusing me of cheating."

"Well, if you can explain that play, go ahead." An even angrier tone.

"I don't have to explain anything to you. Furthermore, I quit."

There was a scuffle of chairs being moved about, the front door slammed, and that was the end of the regular Wednesday night game. It all happened so fast that it didn't make sense. How could adult men who had played together for years let this happen? It couldn't have been just that hand and obviously no one cared to settle the dispute. What they cared about was who would now play for the remainder of the evening.

"Pat, Pat," a familiar voice chirped up the stairs, "wanna help us out and play?" This wasn't my idea of a sterling invitation, but I was curious to see who was left in the game. It was impossible from the upstairs hall to tell the accused from the accuser. As soon as I entered the living room it was apparent, as the accuser was still defending his actions. The remaining other man, Mr. Z., was someone I knew from our club. Someone who consistently turned me off, not on. I always thought of him as loud, aggressive, and messy. But I soon learned through bridge what a decent person he was and through the years I remember him as an important teacher.

For the next several weeks I played regularly with them and each week learned more and more about Mr. Z. For instance, no matter whether he was winning or losing he was always amenable to quitting if someone wanted to leave. Generally the losers request "just one more rubber," which usually takes another hour. But Mr. Z. never pulled that line. His attitude made me take another look at him.

He never bitched about his cards. Another rare quality. It wasn't that he didn't care, but he was a good sport. And a good sport at the table means a good sport in life. He was a generous winner, and one night when he had an especially good win he stuck a dollar in the baby's piggy bank. That told me even more about him. So when he suggested we play with him and his wife I found myself accepting readily. He was not a particularly good player but he was nice. She was slightly below average, but with him as a partner she was cool and comfortable. He never made her feel off balance or insecure. And I particularly liked the way he chided her, not choked her, when she failed to make a contract. No wonder after thirty years they're still married. Mr. Z. opened my eyes to how quickly people can expose themselves through cards. And I've found that no matter how different they may appear away from the table, at the table is what they're all about.

Of all the things he did, there is one in particular that endeared him to me forever. He and his wife had reached a slam. After the opening lead he turned to us and said, "I know I can make this hand if I can use a pencil!"

"What do you mean, use a pencil?" We both giggled.

"Well, I'm going to run all my high cards but I don't think I can remember your discards! So if I can write them down I think I can make it."

"I don't think you're allowed to do that," my husband said, "but we can call a local bridge club and ask."

Bridge clubs are usually very accommodating — sort of the Yellow Pages for cards. It was only a courtesy call, for one of the elements of bridge is to remember the cards. No one has ever come up with a sure-fire way of remembering. I always keep track of the ones unplayed instead of the ones played. You have to find the best way for yourself and stick to it. But first, unclutter your mind. Second, play slowly.

Mr. Z. was right. He needed a pencil, but he had already planted the "I can't make it" thought, so he was down before the opening lead.

This is a progressive squeeze and one of the toughies. Mr. Z. knew the King of Clubs was offside because I had overcalled a Diamond. The play went as follows: The King of Diamonds

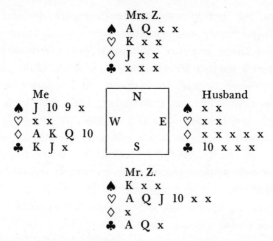

Mrs. Z.
♠ A Q x x
♡ K x x
◇ J x x
♣ x x x

Me
♠ J 10 9 x
♡ x x
◇ A K Q 10
♣ K J x

N
W   E
S

Husband
♠ x x
♡ x x
◇ x x x x x
♣ 10 x x x

Mr. Z.
♠ K x x
♡ A Q J 10 x x
◇ x
♣ A Q x

Opening Lead: Diamond King
Contract: 6 Hearts

was led followed by the Ace, which Mr. Z. trumped. He then
drew trumps in two rounds and cashed two Spades, the King, and
Queen, ending in his hand to play two more trumps. Here is
the end position:

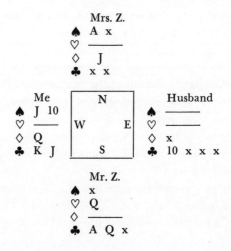

Mrs. Z.
♠ A x
♡ ———
◇ J
♣ x x

Me
♠ J 10
♡ ———
◇ Q
♣ K J

N
W   E
S

Husband
♠ ———
♡ ———
◇ x
♣ 10 x x x

Mr. Z.
♠ x
♡ Q
◇ ———
♣ A Q x

On the last trump I was squeezed in three suits. If I ditched the Queen of Diamonds he could then cross to the table, play the now high Jack of Diamonds, and in making a discard on the Diamond Jack I would be squeezed again. And again. Whatever I chose to discard would produce the same situation. But poor Mr. Z. was so concerned about not remembering he did indeed forget to remember. He laughed after he went down. "See, I told you I could make it with a pencil." No doubt he could have, but his going down and his laugh exposed an insecurity. And his insecurity probably accounted for his being a bit loud socially. Whatever it was, this was another way of covering it up. Surely the head of a successful business could remember a few discards.

As players, take these signs from people at the table and make them work for you. Every time I see a squeeze situation I still think of him, and sometimes wish I had a pencil.

In time the men replaced their fourth, forgot about me, so I went back to playing duplicate. One evening I was gleefully relating the Mr. Z. story to my partner, Irv Fisher, as I arranged the following hand:

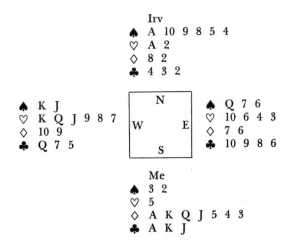

Irv
♠ A 10 9 8 5 4
♡ A 2
◇ 8 2
♣ 4 3 2

♠ K J
♡ K Q J 9 8 7
◇ 10 9
♣ Q 7 5

♠ Q 7 6
♡ 10 6 4 3
◇ 7 6
♣ 10 9 8 6

Me
♠ 3 2
♡ 5
◇ A K Q J 5 4 3
♣ A K J

We reached the fairly good contract of 6 Diamonds, but after the opening lead of the Heart King, all seemed to depend on the Club finesse. In short, there was no squeeze possibility. I thought about Mr. Z., and giggled, looked at the two hands, finessed the Club Queen, and went down one. The play took only three minutes.

"Don't you ever do that again." Irv glared at me. "You simply gave up."

"I don't know what you mean — gave up."

"You took one look at the hand, decided it depended on the finesse, stopped thinking, and went down — in record time," he added.

I could feel the blood beginning to boil. Wasn't there ever an end? "Oh, come on, Irv, let up."

"You just let up enough for both of us," he continued. "Is that how you're going to live your life?"

"My life hasn't got anything to do with it."

"Oh, yes, it does. When you were having labor pains you didn't walk out of the Nationals. And as long as we're on the subject, even your impending divorce shows you're not walking out on your life. You're taking the harder road instead of playing it safe."

Ye Gods, I thought, what's it got to do with bridge? And what's it got to do with this hand? A bit sarcastically I asked, "Okay, what'd I do wrong?"

"You forgot you were playing against human beings, not machines. And human beings make mistakes, so when you need their mistakes give them a chance to make them."

He was right, of course. I thought about "gimme" putts. Playing for fun you give short putts, but never in a tournament. And how many times have you seen an expert miss a two-footer?

"The opponents didn't have a clue about your hand," he continued. "If you had taken your time you might have seen that by running the Diamond suit they would have difficulty making five discards. You could postpone the Club finesse."

Later that night he made me defend with the West hand. After six Diamonds are played, West is in a bind. He cannot see the singleton Heart in my hand and he has no inkling of where the Spade Queen is.

So being West, I followed two rounds of trumps and made four discards, coming to this end position:

> Spades: K J
> Hearts: Q
> Diamonds: none
> Clubs: Q 7 5

What could I discard on the last Diamond? It was indeed a problem.

"Now," continued Irv, "if the West hand does not throw a Club you can resort to the finesse, but meanwhile you have given him a problem."

"That's a phony squeeze!"

"Exactly — a pseudosqueeze."

There are times to bluff, times to concede, times to be strong, and times to be weak. I was learning all of this at the table, and for the next several years was going to need it in life, as well. But, just as important, I think I was going to learn when a pseudosqueeze was being perpetrated against me — and not just at the bridge table.

8—

Fowl Play

"I HAVE NEVER heard of arranging a divorce around a bridge tournament," my old family lawyer said, as he leaned across his desk. Peering over his spectacles he continued, "And I suppose your incompatibility has to do with your bidding?"

"That's part of it. He still squirms whenever I play Notrump, thinks men's games are the greatest, refuses to admit there is something called female intuition, and if I have to travel to Alabama I might as well stay south for the National Tournament in Florida."

All of the above was only half right. You don't get a divorce simply over a bridge game, but you do when the missing ingredients at the table are missing in the house. My husband got custody of the trophy and I got the baby. Seemed reasonable to me.

"Wanna tell me about it?" Naturally my lawyer was a bridger.

"Well, I was playing against my husband. Here's the situation."

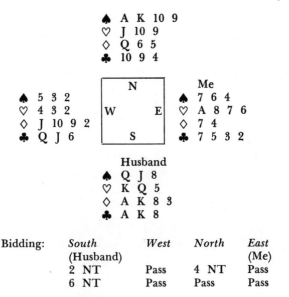

♠ A K 10 9
♡ J 10 9
◇ Q 6 5
♣ 10 9 4

W

♠ 5 3 2
♡ 4 3 2
◇ J 10 9 2
♣ Q J 6

Me

♠ 7 6 4
♡ A 8 7 6
◇ 7 4
♣ 7 5 3 2

Husband

♠ Q J 8
♡ K Q 5
◇ A K 8 3
♣ A K 8

Bidding:	South (Husband)	West	North	East (Me)
	2 NT	Pass	4 NT	Pass
	6 NT	Pass	Pass	Pass

Opening Lead: Jack of Diamonds

The 4 Notrump bid was not Blackwood. It asked the opener to bid slam if the 2 Notrump bid was a good one, a maximum.

My husband won the opening lead with the Ace, tricky but not impossible to read (he stroked it just the way he returned service). He then played the King of Hearts (delivered like his first serve). I saw no reason to win the trick, so I ducked. He rolled his brown eyes in my direction and played the 5 ("Get into the alley"). In one movement he was trying to make me play the Ace, if I held it, so I ducked again. After all, hadn't he taught me to duck on the tennis court? Now if he tried another Heart I could cash the Ace, then set the hand with the thirteenth Heart. Or if by ducking the Heart 5 this gave him his twelfth trick, I couldn't prevent it by taking the Ace. He was executing an important element in a squeeze play: In order to effect a squeeze you have to give up your loser and then start the squeeze.

He cashed four Spades, but West was able to discard a Heart comfortably, waiting to win his Diamond and Club. West could not be squeezed once the original duck of the Heart had been made. For practice, lay out the West cards, have East win the second Heart, and you'll see that the West hand is squeezed.

"What made you duck the Heart?" my husband asked.

"You did."

"I did?"

"Yep, the ball was coming straight at me when I was in the alley and you told me to duck. So when the Heart King came at me it reminded me of the ball."

"Very funny."

"And to quote Mr. Goren, 'At the bridge table as at the dining table, the duck can be a spectacular success.' "

My lawyer shrugged his shoulders. "Men and women," he uttered.

"Women and men." I corrected the order.

"Sometimes you can't win from winning," he reflected.

"I guess that about sums it up. Maybe next time. Anyway, after the divorce in Alabama I'm planning to play at the Nationals in Florida, so that's why I want to make only one trip south."

"You bridge players are crazy."

"Practical." I decided it was best not to tell him that my husband and I had flipped a coin to see who would get to go to the tournament and who'd stay home with the baby. He would probably have committed us instead of divorcing us.

Ten days later I walked into the arena in Miami, single and excited at the prospect of playing a National Tournament without labor pains.

The only playing date I had was with a girlfriend from home, a four-session National Women's Pairs Championship. Men scoff at women's events, but I've yet to meet the man who could qualify for the finals, much less win it. It takes a particular skill to play against the female of the species, and they are by far more deadly than the male.

Midway through the event we arrived with a cheery hello at the table of the defenders, the women who had won the previous year. (We were in second place, so very cheery we were.) Dead silence from them. We picked up our hands and the auction/ action went like this.

1ST DEFENDER (DEALER) : One Club. (She then turned her eyes in the direction of my partner and stared, a hard fierce stare. Her partner, having looked at her cards, joined her in the stare sequence. Four eyes burned into the forehead of my partner. Had she been wax she would have melted.)

PARTNER: Pass. (Fairly audible, considering she had just been singed.)

2ND DEFENDER: One Heart. (She briefly took her eyes off my partner to examine her cards and made the bid with great authority. Then, on cue, all four eyes shifted to my virgin forehead.)

ME: One Spade. (How could I miss the bid with six eyes?)

1ST DEFENDER: *Two Clubs.* (All eyes on my partner.)

PARTNER: Pass. (Retaliating by blowing smoke into the middle of the table.)

2ND DEFENDER: *Two Diamonds.* (And now I really got it — both defenders glared at me and leaned on the table.)

ME: Two Spades. (Four eyes almost fell on the table as I dared to bid again — against them.)

1ST DEFENDER: Paasszz. (Yesterday's sun-tan lotion began to ooze from her pores as her eyes dug into my partner.)

PARTNER: Pass. (Cool, undaunted, with great courage.)

2ND DEFENDER: *DOUBLE!* (We'll get these upstarts.)

ME: Pass. (I had nowhere to go, not even a husband to run to.)

1ST DEFENDER: *I* pass. (How was she spelling I/eye?)

PARTNER: Pass. (She gave me a look: Steady, girl, they're out to get you.)

First Defender plunked down her opening lead, my partner tabled the dummy, 2nd Defender got ready for the vulnerable kill, and I stared at the thirteen cards with a crazy head that went like this: Wonder if this is a simple squeeze? (Take your time.) Maybe it's a pseudosqueeze. (How's the baby?) Duck the first trick? (I'm hungry.) Hold up play? (I lost the key to my room. Well, you can't leave now anyway.) Throw up play? (No, you fool, it's called throw in.)

I managed to return to the table mentally and saw eight top tricks staring me in the face. All I had to do was take them. Any novice could do it. My partner saw me counting and securing the cards — the last thing I wanted to do was drop them on the table — and with complete aplomb she said, "Well, when we arrived at the table we were only six points behind you. If Pat makes this hand we'll be in first place!" Gamesmanship. I could have leaned across the table and kissed her.

I played the hand slowly and carefully as Irv Fisher had taught me, but played it with their eyes on me the whole time. Perhaps their eye movement wasn't cheating or unethical, so to be a good sport I'll call it unsporting. This action had probably worked for them against weak players for years — they certainly had the timing down pat.

A few tricks from the end I managed to raise my eyes and very slowly looked from one to the other, then uttered, "If you don't keep your eyes on your cards I may make an overtrick!" Then they backed off.

About three years later we played against them in New York, and damned if they didn't start it all over again. But like most bridge players, having total recall, they remembered the Miami mishap and retrenched.

Any man wanna try his hand at a Women's event?

Before the final round my partner eased herself into my only easy chair. "Well, guess you can see how tough part-scores are."

"Sure they're tough. I think tournaments are won and lost on part-scores."

"Some of the girls have an edge," she dropped casually.

"What's that mean?"

"Well, they handle their part-score bidding with — caution."

"I think I know what you're saying but I don't think I like it. What do they do?"

"With a healthy raise (One Spade–Two Spades) they keep their eyes on the cards. With an unhealthy raise they look around the room."

"And just where did you pick up that bit of unhealthy information?"

She told me. I wish she hadn't. Through the years I thought I could forget it. Obviously, I couldn't.

"Let's forget we ever had this conversation. However, if any one of the people you've mentioned dares to pull this on me at the table, I want you to know I'll scream my guts out to the authorities."

We lost the Women's Pairs, but *we* lost it. There are always several hands you wish you could do over again, but one in particular stands out.

My partner opened the bidding with 1 Club and I held:

Spades: Q x x
Hearts: J 10 x x
Diamonds: x x x x
Clubs: x x

I will agree that Pass is reasonable, acceptable, book bid, etc., but something bothered me on the back of my neck, so I responded to the alert. One Heart from me. Two Spades from partner. Forcing? Right. Well, I figured as long as we were out of the bad Club fit and in the major-suit fit of at least 4–3 I had done my duty, and so I passed. My partner's glasses slipped to the end of her nose and in a voice that could have been heard in Morocco she said, "How can you pass? It's a forcing bid." Her hand:

> Spades: A K x x
> Hearts: A K x x
> Diamonds: A
> Clubs: A K x x

Obviously a mental block on the opening bid — happens to all of us and usually when we least expect it. But the cute part of the story came about five years later. We were rooming together, not playing together, at a tournament in New York, and after a heavy session I asked her what she would open holding A K x x, A K x x, A, A K x x.

"Aw, come on, Pat, what's the problem? Two Clubs."

"Well, if you had done that five years ago in Miami we would have won the Women's Pairs!"

"You bitch." The only answer she could think of, but said in a loving and friendly way. After all, I had paid her memory a great compliment by waiting so many years.

Bridge players are indeed strange and their memory retention even stranger. I knew I had joined the cult when someone stopped me on the street with a friendly greeting. I couldn't remember his name, but the last time I saw him he was wearing five Spades to the Ace-King, four Hearts to the Queen-Jack, two small Diamonds, and two small Clubs.

The remainder of the Miami National I spent being an observer. I would select a top team to kibitz. You can learn as much by watching as you can by playing, maybe more. The top players are exceedingly disciplined. Armed with all the technical know-how, ready to be applied at a moment's notice, they turn their attention to routine playing. And that difficult four-letter word — Pass. The consistent winners are the mechanical giants. They bid, lead, defend, play the dummy — all with the caution of an atomic bomb mover. Bridge is a game of mistakes. The player who makes the fewest mistakes emerges as the winner. Irv Fisher's very true words.

The postgame sessions, the retelling of hands and stories, are part of the delight of a bridge tournament. And there again the expert differs from the beginner. Never satisfied, the experts will discuss hands on which they scored badly. They will give the problem to others and ask, what would you bid, what lead would you make, what shift do you think is indicated; and they learn and learn from their mistakes. The beginners can usually be heard extolling their successes. Or running from expert to expert asking an opinion about their "partners' " misbids, hopping from player to player until they can find one who agrees with them. Then they run back to their partners with: "See, so-and-so agrees with me." And so, unlike the experts, they have learned nothing.

Experts and nonexperts do have one thing in common. Their egos. The rankest beginner's ego emerges after only a few lessons, and after years of wondering about this I have realized we are all susceptible because we are putting our minds on the line. We are taking our decisions, our judgments, our observations through thought, our thought, and presenting them to the world. And when the world disagrees, *pop* goes the ego.

Two formidable experts, playing as partners, were reviewing the evening's twenty-eight hands, which had been carefully recorded on their personal scorecards. In the margin of his scorecard one expert had noted "EIJ" or "MIS" after certain hands he felt would score badly. His partner, eyeing the penciled notes, asked why MIS was printed by the hands he had played and EIJ after the ones played by his note-making partner.

"Well, the ones you played were mistakes . . . MIS. The ones I played were error in judgment . . . EIJ."

And that ended that expert partnership . . .

9—

The Seven-Year Hitch

MY NEXT SEVEN YEARS were spent in the single experience. If you are a woman and single and you play bridge, you've got it made. There was never a day, night, or weekend that I was alone unless I chose to be.

Bridge can take you anywhere, any time, with or without a partner. Today, bridge cruises leave practically every day for far-off ports or just a three-day outing — depending on your pocketbook, time, and desires. On the cruises I took, after Alfred Sheinwold and I were married, 90 per cent of the players were single. All seemed to have a ball on board, and their love of bridge brought them together and kept them afloat together.

If cruising is not your thing, you can go to duplicate tournaments, which are held practically every night in most cities. Smaller cities run them biweekly. Most country clubs, as well as the Y's and smaller clubs, have installed duplicate events.

Partnerships are not a problem either. If you phone the director of any club and request a partner for the evening, it can almost always be arranged. And in most cases if you appear partnerless, there is usually another loner just waiting for you.

Then there are the rubber bridge clubs. Most big cities have two or three, smaller towns at least one. But they are there, listed in any phone book. Even if you bump into a city where the club is privately owned, courtesy is usually extended to out-of-towners.

All you need is the desire to play; anywhere in the world your wish can be granted. This makes bridge unique. And much easier than horseback-riding or squash. And you've always got your equipment, haven't you? Your intact brain and diminutive ego.

As I approached bridge sans husband I had part of my equipment, my brain. My ego hadn't shrunk to its proper size yet. It had been carefully trodden on in the early years; maybe I permitted it, but at that time I didn't know the difference between permitting and relishing. When I wasn't needed at home and wanted relaxation (?), I sought out the various avenues of bridge. Irv Fisher had moved to Florida, Charlie Schapiro had died, I was too good for the chauffeur, Kirby, who had retired after my father's death anyhow. For a fleeting moment I thought about remarrying my husband for Mixed Pairs events but had to discard that when he married one of my ex–Women's Pairs partners! So it was go it alone — freedom from the known.

Usually during a weekend tournament the Women's Pairs single-session event is played the first day, followed by the Mixed Pairs at night. The following two days never presented a problem as the events were open; any combination was acceptable. So I found myself playing in Washington, D.C., on a snowy afternoon in the Women's Pairs with one of my all-time favorite partners, Terry Michaels. Terry had no Mixed Pairs–partner problem because her husband, Mike, was just a few feet away playing in the Men's Pairs. Sometime during the session a strange man approached our table, asked if I were free for the Mixed Pairs that evening, and, thinking Mike Michaels had sent him over, I too quickly said yes. He mumbled something about dinner so we could discuss our systems and strategy, and I mumbled back yes, searching Terry's eyes for a clue. But she was buried in Diamonds and Clubs. We agreed on twenty minutes to clean up before dinner, and I told him I'd meet him in front of the dining room. He corrected this — the coffee shop.

I slapped some water on my face, combed my hair, waved good-bye to my roommate, and headed for the coffee shop. My first date as a single bridger.

"How'd you and Terry make out today?" was his opening gambit.

"Very well, thank you. We won."

"Well, let's make it two in a row for you tonight."

I liked that. It's always a good idea to enter an event planning to win, so his attitude was well placed. We discussed our approach to the various systems, which went like this.

HIM: How do you play your Notrumps?

ME (refraining from the smart-ass answer of "Well"): Sixteen to eighteen.

HIM: Okay. Stayman?

ME: Fine. Not forcing.

HIM: Forcing (just like his tone).

ME: Forcing — I hope I remember.

WAITRESS: How do you want your hamburger?

ME: Medium.

HIM (to the waitress): We'll both take it rare. (To me): It's better for your energy level.

ME: Uh-huh.

HIM: What kind of overcalls do you play?

ME: Weak.

HIM: Medium.

ME: No, that's how I like my hamburger.

HIM: What kind of Two bids?

ME: Two Clubs only force?

HIM: Strong (as indeed he was — forcing and strong).

ME: Do you like Texas?

HIM: Nope, I'm a Yankee through and through.

ME (forget about Texas — the last time you played it was a disaster anyway): Okay.

HIM: I use Blackwood. Don't like Gerber.

ME: I hope Mr. Gerber doesn't hear you say that. He's really a lovely man.

HIM: Want some dessert?

ME: What do you think would be good for me? (wising up).

HIM: Jell-O.

ME: Mighty fine.

HIM: No, that brand isn't as good as regular Jell-O.

ME: Very funny.

HIM: Check, please.

ME: Please — let me split it with you.

HIM: No, we can discuss it later. More important to get our signals straight.

So our convention card read like this:

> *Notrumps:* 16–18, Stayman forcing
> *Overcalls:* Medium
> *Two Bids:* Strong
> *Others:* Blackwood

Simple as A, B, C. We took our places at the table after I offered to pay my own entry fee (only two dollars in those days), but he refused. Again, he said we'd discuss it later. Terry passed by and I waited for her to greet my partner, but instead she waited for an introduction. I was not only wrong about Stayman, Texas, Gerber, overcalls, opening 2 bids, meat, and Jell-O, but about my partner. Well, when Mike came in he would know him. Wrong. Mike just walked by with a wave in my direction. Everyone thought he was a new beau I had imported for the occasion. Later I found out my friends had several partners in mind for me but were being, oh, so circumspect when they saw me with — I've forgotten his name.

There was something different about this Mixed Pairs and it took me a while to comprehend it. Up until now I had played these events with my ex, not taking too much notice of the other women. But as I sat there in my afternoon attire (best cashmere sweater and matching skirt), I observed that the others were all gussied up. Before World War II, I had been told, players dressed on Saturday nights for the finals of the Open Pairs, but the custom had been dropped. The directors, however, still dressed, making them look elegant as well as official. But these ladies were really put together. I let it pass; maybe they were going out afterward.

My partner opened the bidding with 1 Club. I responded 1 Notrump, holding 9 high-card points and no four-card major. He looked uncomfortable and passed. We made 2 for a high score.

"I think it would be better if you just bid one Diamond so I could bid the Notrump," he chided.

"But it only makes one from your side of the table. You'll get a different lead."

"Better strategy," he countered. "People think women are a pushover when they play Notrump; they're more afraid of men."

I thought I would push him over — over on the floor.

He played the next few hands, so I relaxed with a Camel and began to appraise the situation. The pairs were slowly being catalogued in my mind.

1. Expert marrieds, such as Terry and Mike Michaels, who could be playing together in any event. These expert pairs disagreed at times, but their discussion was held to a discussion, without the "I'll get even with you" attitude.

2. Men and women married to each other who were not experts but regular players. They screamed and yelled, asserting

themselves and never agreeing on the problem. Needless to say, they are still at the same point twenty years later, which is why they are not experts.

3. Men who played regularly, but never with their wives, except in these Mixed Pairs events. Their wives, in turn, looked forward to this, but God knows why. With each bid they were scolded or reprimanded or made to feel like dull dishwater. These women would have been better off partnered by strangers. They would have played better, been treated better, and enjoyed the game better. But there they were, clinging to their masters' every word — right or wrong. I could only gather that they were accustomed to this type of behavior away from the table, too, and enjoyed it.

4. The love-in couples. Everything they do works out. If they have ten finesses to take on one hand — watch out. All ten will work. If they are in 3 Notrump and it should go down one when 4 Hearts is cold, they will make 4 Notrump and you'll end up with a rotten score. Cupid hovers over them, shooting hearts into their cards and darts into yours. Just sit back and be prepared to go to the cleaners, and thank God if the bidding goes Pass, Pass, Pass, Pass, when they're at your table.

5. The affluent ladies bent on becoming Life Masters. Their only hope is to pay an expert to play with them. Now this requires a special skill from the expert. He has several things to do. One, he must manage to play most of the hands. Two, he prays he will be on lead most of the time when the opponents are playing. Three, he has to keep a civil tongue in his head. Four, he has to watch out for her mistakes and gently try to suggest another line of play or bid (never criticize). This is tricky because a bridge player's voice level, when reviewing a hand, is usually at the top of the dial. Five, he must constantly be in the final top ten or lovely lady will take her business elsewhere to win her Master Points.

6. The gals who want a sleep-in after the play-in. They are

the gussied-up ones. This scenario had eluded me before tonight. The caliber of their bridge could range from beginner to advanced intermediate. They are lonely, enjoy bridge to an extent, but have discovered that the world of bridge-playing males outranks women about six to one. Pretty good odds.

I was sitting there, mentally filing all of this information away, when I observed Dick Freeman walking up and down the aisles. Dick had been one of the original Quiz Kids from Chicago and now was a tournament director as well as a fine player. With a few minutes between rounds, I casually asked him what he was doing.

"Just checking out the future opposition," he answered, as if it were the normal thing to do.

"You mean you file this away for future reference?"

"Yep," he went on, walking from table to table, "we play against these people so often it helps to know their habits."

Chewing on my lower lip, I sauntered back to the table. He's right, I thought. Personal habits at the table are as important as cleaning your teeth. I started looking around at the couples against whom we had already played and started a filing cabinet of my own.

1. The expert marrieds. Bid and play your cards as carefully as possible. Remember, they will reach the optimum contract or give you the best defense. Don't look for fancy leads or shaky contracts against them. They will make the most of it. Tight bridge.

2. The married good players. Each sees himself as better than the other and is hell bent on proving it. About 75 per cent of the time they will reach the optimum contract, but be on guard for the hands they bid when a misfit is obvious. They will not demur but fight it out. Recognize this situation and take full advantage of it. If you and your partner are in a close spot, such as to bid game or not, be aware of how they are getting along. If they've had a good result on the previous hand they

will play this one well against you. If the previous one was a disaster — then step out and bid the game. Chances are they will slip in the defense or opening lead, as these kinds of players always carry over their grudges.

3. Husbands playing with wives out of duty. If the wife is playing the hand you can afford to do the normal thing, because her insecurity will give you all the advantage you need. If he is playing you can count on some smart-aleck attempt to cover up either the wrong contract or the wrong bid he has made. You can afford to overbid because he will be trying to make up for what he thinks will be her lousy defense.

4. The love-in couples. If you're not lucky enough for the bidding to have gone All Pass, play it close to the chest. These star-crossed lovers have everything going for them. If your hand is a laydown, it's nine to five *you'll* renege! Bless them and get away from the table as fast as possible. Example. Years later when Alfred and I were engaged I opened the bidding with 1 Notrump. Alfred and Edgar Kaplan had devised a system (known strangely enough as Kaplan-Sheinwold), the backbone of which was weak Notrumps, 12–14 points. Alfred and I were not playing his system, which I promptly forgot when I opened the bidding with only 12 points. Alfred, thinking I had at least 16, properly popped me into a small slam, holding 17 points in his engaged hand. There we were — off the first three Diamond tricks! But we were engaged — a love-in couple. The opponents didn't find the Diamond lead (they didn't have a chance), and we racked up 6 Notrump. Cupid does not play favorites. He just flies around, doing his thing for all.

5. The expert and "I gotta be a Life Master-er." Pay a lot of attention to the bidding. The expert will be angling for the right to play the hand. He may bid a suit he doesn't have, he may double to confuse the issue, or he may lie back and enter the auction at the 4 level. He will be operating constantly. If you have the cards, play it straight and right on the mark. He is

good enough to bounce you off the wall even though the lady is just his patroness.

6. The would-be sleep-ins. They fall midway between the love-ins and the duty pairs. Cupid sends his assistants on this job, and like all assistants they take numerous coffee breaks. The males are doing their thing out of duty in order to reap the later rewards. So you have to play it loose and close. If they approach your table all smiles — play it close. If she comes to the table first and he's belting one down in the bar between rounds you can afford to be loose.

These mixed-couple-isms apply to rubber bridge, too. If you play regularly with any of the above, the rules will still help. Get to know your opponents — what makes them tick — and you'll find yourself winning a lot more than you used to. Don't be fooled by one lucky hand. If your regulars overbid regularly, then file it away and use it. If they are chronic underbidders, use this too. Don't make just one more bid and push them into a game they wouldn't bid on their own.

Dick Freeman was right. As long as I lived in the Washington-Baltimore area I would be playing against the same couples in every tournament, so like him, I was filing away notes for the future.

Meanwhile Yankee had finished playing the hand, I had finished my Camel, and we were off and running to the final board.

Male Love-in led their favorite suit — Hearts, the Jack. Yankee played the Ace and without breaking stride cashed the Ace-King of trumps. When he gave up the lead to the Diamond Ace, Mr. Love-in cashed the Queen and Jack of Spades and Ms. Love-in rattled off four Heart tricks for down four, vulnerable, for a miserable score. Figures. Mr. and Ms. Love-in signed the score and toddled off to more bliss, leaving a bloody mess behind. Yankee looked as though a Sherman tank had just rolled across his chest, leaving it like the dinner Jell-O heap.

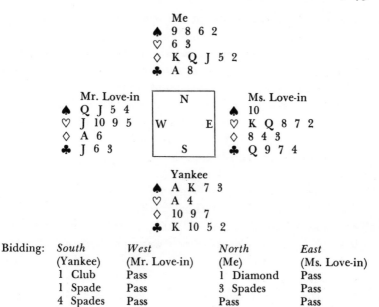

Me
♠ 9 8 6 2
♡ 6 3
◇ K Q J 5 2
♣ A 8

Mr. Love-in
♠ Q J 5 4
♡ J 10 9 5
◇ A 6
♣ J 6 3

Ms. Love-in
♠ 10
♡ K Q 8 7 2
◇ 8 4 3
♣ Q 9 7 4

Yankee
♠ A K 7 3
♡ A 4
◇ 10 9 7
♣ K 10 5 2

Bidding:	South	West	North	East
	(Yankee)	(Mr. Love-in)	(Me)	(Ms. Love-in)
	1 Club	Pass	1 Diamond	Pass
	1 Spade	Pass	3 Spades	Pass
	4 Spades	Pass	Pass	Pass

"Wow, what a trump break" was all he could manage to say. He knew this last hand had placed us somewhere between average and underaverage in the final standings. Had he prepared himself for the onslaught he could have salvaged the hand, for the contract was reasonable but the play was not. When you are in an acceptable contract other players will be there with you. So if you think the hand might fail, at least lose it profitably. Even if you have to go all out to make it, try to take the best of all possible ways.

Yankee should have worried about the trump suit and the Heart suit. After winning the opening lead he should cash the trump King and then play *low* to the dummy. If the trumps break he is now in control of the hand; if the trumps break badly (and we know that playing against love-ins it will), he will still have control. West can win only two trumps, one Heart, and the Ace of Diamonds for down one — instead of down four. It's called cutting your losses to the lowest possible number. When you lead low to the dummy, West will probably step up with the trump Jack, but the Heart suit cannot be run against you.

I offered my hand to Yankee, thanked him for the game and dinner, and prepared to settle down with the late show (I've always found it a great way to unwind after bridge). Nothing was farther from his mind.

"Your room or mine?" he said, clutching my outstretched hand.

"Thanks, but the only nightcaps I use are on my head."

"I don't think you understand," still with my hand in his. Terry and Mike walked by, thinking we were holding hands. They smiled, I grimaced to show it was a death grip, not a love clasp. They went away.

"Understand what?" (calling a spade a spade).

"Now the fun of Mixed Pairs starts," persevered Yankee.

"It does? I thought we were having fun all night. Four Spades down four, Three Notrump down three, Six Hearts down six." I pried my hand loose and edged away. And then it came.

"Look, little lady, I bought you dinner, paid your entry, played with you —"

"You what?" I couldn't believe my ears. "I guess you should get points for letting me play Notrump, too."

"Just what do you think Mixed Pairs are all about?" He raised his voice.

I had seventeen answers, couldn't think of one, refrained from slapping him in the face, and fled from the room. With luck (not a good sense of direction) I found the elevator, and got off on the wrong floor. I thrust my key into the lock, which of course didn't budge until it was opened from the inside. Lucky me — I had selected a conventioneer.

"Come right in, I've been waiting for you all my life," he yawned.

"Do you play bridge?" I asked.

"No, but I'm game for a little strip poker."

"Sorry. I only know bridge," and I fled down the hall.

Out in the stairwell I collected myself. First by repeating my name, address, and phone number. Then by checking the name and number on my room key, which assured me I was in the right hotel and if I climbed three more flights my room would be there. Grumbling all the way, I reprimanded myself for behaving like a schoolgirl. If you're old enough to have a baby and a divorce, you are old enough to handle one lone Yankee with hot pants.

By the time I reached the room I was in perfect control of myself. There was no problem when I was greeted with the Do Not Disturb sign on my own door! Tillie, my roomie, was having her own tryst and in a note taped to the door asked if I'd come back in a few hours. Being in complete control, I sat down on the floor a few doors away and began to cry.

A pair of feet with trousers above them came trudging along and asked what I was doing on the floor.

"Crying," I answered, without looking up.

"Surely your game wasn't that bad?" the trousers asked.

"No," the floor sitter responded.

"Then what's wrong?" He sat down next to me. And do you believe I gave him a blow-by-blow description of the whole thing, starting with that damned rare hamburger. He gave me a miniature pack of Kleenex, TLC, and there we sat with my runny nose and running mouth fighting for equal time.

When I finished my story he promised he would punish Yankee next time they met at the bridge table by setting him at least five tricks. So naturally I agreed to have a drink with him.

10—

Slightly Unhitched

AND THAT'S HOW I met Sidney Silodor of Philadelphia. Gentle, kind Sidney, who became one of my closest friends until his untimely death in 1963. *The Official Encyclopedia of Bridge* lists him as "one of the world's greatest players, writer, instructor, bridge lecturer, and lawyer." All true, plus husband, father, golfer, and good friend.

It was Sidney who lifted me off the floor and took me into the higher echelons of bridgedom. That night he was on his way to a small gathering of bridgers and took me along. The room read like a *Who's Who in Bridge,* and because I was with Sidney acceptance was immediate. Most had played in the Mixed Pairs, the very one I had just sat through, and they were busily engaged in discussing the hands. Quickly I whipped out my private score to compare my results with theirs. Through their discussion of bids, leads, and plays, it was easy to see where I had gone wrong and why. I wasn't the least bit concerned about Yankee's mistakes, only my own. That was step number 2 up the progress ladder. When the real love of the game takes over, self-improvement becomes uppermost. To dwell on the mistakes of your partner is a waste of time.

Dave Warner, another Philadelphian, good player, and fantastic raconteur, was sitting in the room and told one of the funniest Mixed Pairs stories I have ever heard. A couple came to his table and had a four-minute bidding sequence finally ending up in a small slam. Dave told us that the bidding became so complicated at the 3 level that each opponent was asked to leave the table after a bid so the partner could explain what he or she thought the bid meant. (This is not uncommon in tournament play, where many systems are used.) The reason the player making the unusual bid is asked to leave the table rather than give the explanation is to prevent him from explaining it to his partner, who just might be as confused as you. So there were Dave and his partner sitting through this complicated mess of bids that resulted in a small slam going down one — off two Aces! Then he said the two players started screaming and yelling, each explaining that the other had misconstrued his bids. While all this was going on Dave turned the duplicate board around (they still had another hand to play), but instead of playing the new hand he just switched the direction of the old one, giving the man the girl's hand and vice versa! Both were probably too annoyed to recognize the hands, and the bidding proceeded just as it had five minutes before. The man made *every* bid the girl had made and the girl made *every* bid the man had made. Only this time Dave and his partner did not ask for explanations, just let them romp ahead.

"What happened, what happened?" We were all screaming by now.

Dave with a perfectly straight face answered, "This time we doubled them. And they left the table never knowing what had happened."

Later that night Dave had to go to the director and tell him what happened to insure that the other players' scores would not suffer because of it. Can you imagine being so annoyed with your partner that you fail to recognize a bidding situation that occurred only five minutes before? If your answer is yes, then back to page one for you!

I accepted a drink, laughed along with the others, and thanked my lucky stars to be out of Yankee's clutches and bids. And even hoped Tillie was enjoying herself.

The stories and gaiety continued until the players had unwound and sleep would be possible. It's a congenial way to keep the Hearts and Spades out of your thoughts when your head hits the pillow. Rest is important, as physical stamina is a vital part of tournament bridge, just as in tennis, golf, or any other sport. Later on, when I was playing regularly in National Tournaments, some preparation was necessary before sitting down to play for ten days, eight hours a day. One of the tournaments was held in Mexico City, where it took us a week to acclimate to the altitude before attempting to compete (just as the Olympic athletes had done prior to the demands of their competition).

Although men have dominated bridge for many years, they are not any better suited to it than their female counterparts. It is perhaps one of the few sports where masculinity and femininity are equal. Harvard has not come up with any statistics to prove the male brain has more cells, so why the underling role of women in bridge?

In the inner sanctum of bridge that night it was apparent that the males were in control. Most of the stories involved a slight belittling of women, but there we sat, listening. In one corner of the room was Helen Sobel, certainly one of the all-time great players and the regular partner of Charles Goren. One time a kibitzer asked, "What does it feel like to play with an expert?" Helen replied, "Ask him."

Although she played often and won with women, like the women of her time, she played with men in the so-called bigger and more prestigious events. Edith Kemp of Florida was also there. She was making a name for herself, but again she played the Open Pairs and Open Teams with men. The famous Josephine Culbertson was partnered by her husband, Ely. Sally Young, Ruth Sherman, Margaret Wagar, to name a few, had established themselves, but women as a whole were not considered a threat.

If the men consciously or unconsciously were categorizing us, we were doing nothing to discourage it. We were allowing ourselves to be ridiculed, almost apologizing for winning any Women's Pairs. Very slowly women began to emerge as the fine players they are, and like their sisters only hit their stride with the advent of Women's Lib. In November of 1975 finally an all-female team played in the coveted Reisinger Team Championship of the Winter Nationals. And almost won. But in the fifties and early sixties we were necessities for Mixed Pairs and the targets of "sure tops" if partnered together in other open events.

Sylvia Stein of Detroit and I opted to play in the Life Masters Pairs in the Summer Nationals in the early sixties. A few boards from the end in the final round, word leaked out that we were leading. I slipped into the corridor for a drink of water and overheard a group of men discussing our position. One said, "If two women win this event I will give up bridge!" We did not win but finished very high, which was very encouraging to others who deep down in their hearts preferred women as their partners.

Rixi Markus of England is a good example. She has been a frontrunner for women in bridge both at the table and at the typewriter. Her skill and ingenuity kept her out of the hands of the Nazis, but never out of the stardom of bridge, usually partnered with — Mrs. Fritzi Gordon.

But there were only a handful in those days, and it behooved us gals to work it out for ourselves before the Betty Friedans and Gloria Steinems. And I wasn't doing too well. Conditioned by or believing in the fiction, I continued my search for a Mixed Pairs partner.

Instead of a snowy afternoon in Washington, D.C., it was a rainy afternoon in Wilmington, Delaware. Terry was sitting opposite me when a note was delivered.

"You have the most gorgeous arms. Could we play in the Mixed Pairs this evening?" signed North #10.

A quick glance to North #10 produced Tillie. Surely she wasn't interested in my arms.

"Your bid." My right-hand opponent smiled sweetly.

"Two arms," I said. Even cool Terry looked up. Her partner had freaked out.

"Is that a new convention?" Right-hand opponent smiled viciously (maybe the men were right).

I corrected it. "I bid Ten Norths." Terry undauntedly asked me to try again. The right-hand opponent called the director. This move is generally made when an out-of-order procedure takes place. (Actually they were in order — I bid Arms first, then North 10.)

As Mike Goldstein, directeur propre, approached the table, he could not hear me telling the ladies to be careful because I was sleeping with him. Terry promptly choked on her coffee. She knew that Mike and I had probably exchanged twenty words in two years. Innocent Mike asked what had happened and the opponents repeated the auction. Their looks of "We know you will rule in *her* favor" went unnoticed by him but not my left-eyed winking. I showed him the note to explain my nonsensical bids, he gave me a brief ruling and winked back (dear boy that he is), and we tried again.

The ladies left the table and I explained the note to Terry. Her only comment was — and I love her for it — "What good are two gorgeous arms if they can't propel the cards in the right order?" Terry and I had one of those zany relationships, which through the years proved to be a very successful one at the table as well as away from it. Terry taught me how to be a pro at the table. Once, in the midst of a turbulent love affair many years later, I walked into the finals of the United States Women's Team Championship partnered by Terry and teammates Muriel Kaplan and Pauline Schmuckler of Philadelphia. We were leading the field, but I was very dismayed by the previous night's contretemps with my amour. Terry looked at me and said in a very firm voice, "Pat, we are engaged in a National Tournament. We are here to win. I will be happy to discuss your problem later, but this is the time for your full attention on bridge or you shouldn't be playing."

And she was right. She backed herself up later in the day when we discovered we had lost by one board. One of our teammates, in an effort to exonerate herself from a disaster, offered the excuse that she had not heard the bidding. Terry said, "You do not *not* hear the bidding in a National Tournament." Again, she was right. In tennis it would be like closing your eyes when you receive service.

North #10, seated in the Men's Pairs, asked me to dinner. This time I was smart and said I'd meet him in front of the coffee shop twenty minutes after the game. He corrected this — the dining room. (Terry said I was finally coming up in the world.) And once again we discussed our system.

> *Notrumps:* 15 plus to 18 minus
> *Overcalls:* Weak
> *Two Bids:* Weak
> *Others:* Texas

Definitely an improvement over the one with Yankee. Simple as A, B, C, and now D.

We took our places at the table, North #10, me, and my gorgeous arms. I was a bit self-conscious about them as they lit cigarettes, reached for cups of black coffee, and initialed scores — all part of bridge. We were in a delicious 6 Notrump contract.

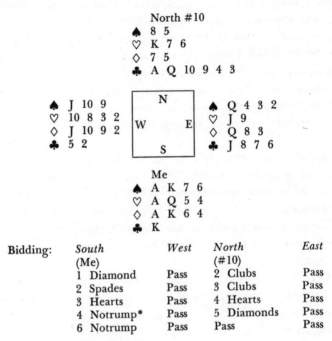

North #10
♠ 8 5
♡ K 7 6
◇ 7 5
♣ A Q 10 9 4 3

♠ J 10 9
♡ 10 8 3 2
◇ J 10 9 2
♣ 5 2

W   E

♠ Q 4 3 2
♡ J 9
◇ Q 8 3
♣ J 8 7 6

Me
♠ A K 7 6
♡ A Q 5 4
◇ A K 6 4
♣ K

Bidding:

	South (Me)	West	North (#10)	East
	1 Diamond	Pass	2 Clubs	Pass
	2 Spades	Pass	3 Clubs	Pass
	3 Hearts	Pass	4 Hearts	Pass
	4 Notrump*	Pass	5 Diamonds	Pass
	6 Notrump	Pass	Pass	Pass

Opening Lead: Diamond Jack

The opening lead was won in my hand with the Diamond King. We were in a good contract, and if the Clubs split, thirteen tricks were mine for the gathering. My bare but beautiful arm laid down the Club King as the lady on my right said, "Oh, it's you! I thought *you'd* be playing with the director!" My beautiful right arm gathered in the 3 of Clubs from the dummy as I glared at her. The 4 of Hearts to the King provided me with the entry to the dummy to run (huh?) the remainder of

* Blackwood.

the Clubs. Much to my horror they did not split, and I was rewarded for being one of those dumb broads the guys in the back room were always talking about. I sat there with my equally dumb face hanging out (and those ugly arms). My partner had a look of consternation on his face; he never raised his eyes, never spoke a word, just sat there staring hard at the dummy. It's a terrible feeling to take ten tricks instead of twelve — especially when you've said you'd take twelve. There was nothing to do but go down gracefully. The proper play is to overtake the Club King with the Ace. This provides you with the safety play against the odds of the suit breaking 4–2. And after the 10 loses to the Jack you can reenter the dummy with the Heart King to cash your now good Clubs. My partner asked me if I would step into the hall after the hand. Was he going to beat me? I apologized for the mental aberration, but he said what I did afterward was worse. Not understanding, I asked for an explanation.

"Never do that again. Never." I looked at him with the blankest face in all bridgedom.

"I hope I'll never do that again," I said.

"That's not what I mean. When you have locked yourself out of the dummy don't give up. Take a few seconds, light a cigarette, give the opponents a chance to make a mistake. Play from the wrong hand and if they cover the trick you are home."

There was no point in asking for any further explanation. He thinks what he said is part of the game; I think it's cheating. There's something called legal larceny in bridge — comes about without malice or premeditation. It's just partnership understanding after years of playing together. One learns from constant exposure to one's regular partner how she or he will resolve certain situations. For example, in a given bidding situation where partner can go one way or the other you know which way he will go — from his previous handling of the same situation. This is not cheating, but the huge advantage of playing regularly with the same person. Just like when your spouse scratches his head with his left hand you know he's about to launch into the story about the traveling salesman.

Sometimes constant exposure to opponents can bring about the same results. Sidney Silodor played often with Norman Kay, stockbroker, world champion, and fellow Philadelphian. Norman is a sweet guy who always inquires about your health and the kids before slipping the knife into you at the table — but he slips it because of his great skill. However, having played against him for years, I now know that when Norman says, "I double you," you have a fifty-fifty chance of making the hand. But when Norman, who has a slight stammer, says, "I d-d-d-double you," you are going down at least 500 points!

Husbands and wives have the greatest opportunities playing together but seldom take advantage of it. The sound of your spouse's voice must be so familiar to you. The voice that opens the door in the evening with a cheery hello tells you either the market went up eight points or he got a raise. You can recognize the symptoms from the kitchen. So why not at the table? It's the same guy. The one reading the morning newspaper who only answers in ughs and ahs is the one who can't decide whether to raise your suit or bid his again. In the great language of bidding you have to determine whether your spouse is speaking classical Greek or baby talk. But there you are with all of those hidden treasures working for you at the table. The next time you are about to explode, listen a little more carefully, take the imaginary cotton out of your ears.

The message I was getting from Mixed Pairs partner North #10 was loud and clear. I listened, didn't like, said goodnight, and went in search of Sidney. It became apparent that if I were ever to play with him it would be a chance outing. He played the big events with Norman Kay, and the lesser events he had to play with his pupils. It also became apparent that if I were to play with better unattached male players in the Mixed events they would have to be talked into it or gently persuaded that their reputations would not be diminished by sitting down in a Mixed Pairs event.

The second year of the seven-year hitch being unhitched I kept a personal scorecard of my partners:

Mixed Pairs:

    Ezra in Easton:

        Weak Notrumps

        Weak jump overcalls

        Weak Two bids

        Weak-weak-weak everythings including our score (made late show with ease — he was too weak to chase)

    Luke in Lancaster:

        Down six in six!

        (Late for late show buying six-pack)

    Adam in Atlantic City:

        He bid Spades — 4 times

        I bid Hearts — 4 times

        He won.

        (Late show — *The Misfits*)

The Pep Boys:

    Manny: Only heard of high-low in poker.

    Moe: Thinks a dummy reversal is when the dummy gets up and plays the cards.

    Jack: Leads fourth from longest and strongest but counts up not down!

Miscellaneous:

    Tom: Squeezes wrong Queens.

    Dick: Sits on Ace, plays like ass.

    Harry: Gin — his real game.

    Luigi: Thinks ashorta club is a misdeal!

And then . . .

I wandered to the drinking fountain during the half-time break and there he was. Tall, dark, handsome, and a bridge player — I could tell by the mangled pencil in his mouth. He offered me his cup of water, I offered him a bit of advice: "Pencils are cheaper today. You might die of cheap lead poisoning and that would be a shame." Four rounds later he appeared at our table. He was even more attractive at the table than he was at the water fountain. He was polite and courteous to his female partner but I couldn't categorize them — I was too busy categorizing me. If he could play bridge then we could be a love-in couple who played both games well. The first board went four passes. Couldn't learn much from that but he did pass with great élan. And then the second board.

```
                        ♠ A Q
                        ♡ K Q 6 5
                        ◇ Q 8 7
                        ♣ J 8 6 2
                   ┌──────────────┐      Me
  ♠ K J 8 5 4 2    │      N       │   ♠ 10 9 7 3
  ♡ 4 3            │ W         E  │   ♡ A J 7 2
  ◇ 6 5 2          │              │   ◇ 4 3
  ♣ 9 5            │      S       │   ♣ 7 4 3
                   └──────────────┘
                        Sexpert
                        ♠ 6
                        ♡ 10 9 8
                        ◇ A K J 10 9
                        ♣ A K Q 10
```

Bidding:	South	West	North	East
	(Sexpert)			(Me)
	1 Diamond	Pass	1 Heart	Pass
	2 Clubs	Pass	4 Clubs	Pass
	4 Hearts	Pass	4 Spades	Pass
	4 Notrump	Pass	5 Diamonds	Pass
	6 Notrump	Pass	Pass	Pass

Aggressive and definitely a Mixed Pairs bid. My partner

somehow found the 4 of Hearts opening lead. Ms. Dummy beamingly laid down her cards. It took Sexpert only a few seconds to sum up his problem: the location of the Heart Ace or the Spade King for his twelfth trick. Deftly he played the Heart King, turning his liquid brown eyes in my direction, imploring me to play the Ace if I held it.

Our eyes never parted, my fingers found their way to the 2 of Hearts; softly it hit the table. As he reached for the 8 in his hand, his eyes thanked me. He was so grateful. To further show his gratitude he proceeded to squeeze the hell out of us. With each Diamond attack I felt his arms tightening around my quivering body. On the third Diamond round I discarded the Heart 7 to prove my undying loyalty. On the fourth and fifth Diamonds, two Club discards from me. (He must know I am relieving him of any Club guess.) Trustingly he switched to Clubs after the last Diamond. Dutifully I dropped the 7 . . . my last Club, my love. I have given you the perfect count, my prince.

As he persevered with the Clubs I couldn't resist placing the Spade King for him. A simple high-low signal.

Then he paused.

I went cold.

He looked at the dummy.

Could he see through my cards? I felt nude.

Should I light a cigarette? No, no movement, only uninterrupted breathing, keeping the stride. I looked longingly into his eyes. Your room or mine, they were imploring.

He played from his hand — a low Heart . . .

From the bed my Heart pounded as he poured two glasses of champagne. Finally a Mixed Pairs partner, a bridge player, a gorgeous hunk of man! No more Yankees, no more mysterious North #10s, no more Mannys or Moes or Jacks of Spades . . . Master of none.

After the first glass of champagne he suggested a bath. Well, if I had executed a Bath Coup on him, turnabout is fair play. Sliding around in the Vita bath suds he stroked my body as deftly as he stroked the dummy.

Back in bed his demands were strong, no weak preempts, no wishy-washy overcalls. Every finesse worked, simple squeezes were child's play, progressive squeezes expertly handled — no need for pseudoanything, all four hands were exposed.

When it was his turn to call he never passed. He made his contract with three overtricks.

After the final session (there was no doubt he'd qualify), he dressed to leave. In my soporific state I asked him who the dummy was at our table.

"That was no dummy, darling (darling — seven beautiful letters — grand slam — seven, the magic number), that was my wife!"

Speaking of double dummies . . .

11—

Swinging Chickens and Rocking-Chair Chic

WHY DOES THE CHICKEN cross the road? Why do we do any of the things we do? What are our reasons, our motives? How often, if ever, do we ever examine them? Maybe the chicken is curious. Or maybe the chicken is bored on his side and thinks the other is better. Does he cross with the light or does he live dangerously, trying to beat the oncoming car?

The way a person plays bridge has a lot in common with that chicken. Your reasons and motives will eventually dictate how well you play the game. And perhaps a little insight into your reasons will explain why you miss signals, get tired easily, or just don't give a damn.

Let's take a look at a typical afternoon game. For starters, if it's an afternoon game the players are mainly passing time. Housewives with children in school and waiting to start dinner, semiretired men waiting to go home for dinner, college students either between classes or avoiding some unpleasant chore. When they arrive at the table they have told you this much about themselves. And so will their playing.

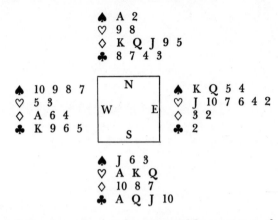

♠ A 2
♡ 9 8
◇ K Q J 9 5
♣ 8 7 4 3

♠ 10 9 8 7
♡ 5 3
◇ A 6 4
♣ K 9 6 5

♠ K Q 5 4
♡ J 10 7 6 4 2
◇ 3 2
♣ 2

♠ J 6 3
♡ A K Q
◇ 10 8 7
♣ A Q J 10

North and South arrive at the reasonable contract of 3 Notrump. And West gets off to the equally reasonable lead of the
Spade 10. It doesn't matter what South does with the lead. If it
is ducked (the defense will continue the Spades) or if South
decides to win the trick, either way the sure entry to the Diamond suit is gone. So let's assume you duck, the defense plays
another Spade, and there you are. If the Spades are divided 4–4
you can simply lose the Diamond Ace and take your nine tricks.
So you play the Diamond King, East plays the 3, and good old
West hops in with the Ace. West, out for an outing, is paying
no attention to his partner's discard. He is securely wrapped in
the blanket of the King of Clubs — the setting trick, he thinks:
three Spades, Ace of Diamonds, and just sit back with the King
of Clubs to defeat the contract. Very lazy thinking on a lazy
afternoon.

First of all, West should haul out his pocket calculator. His
hand contains 7 high-card points, and his partner is known to
have 5 — the King and Queen of Spades. Declarer has opened
1 Notrump so has at least 16 points, making a total of 38 points
(including dummy's 10) out of 40. (Counting all high cards
with their proper value, each deck contains 40 high-card points.)

The most partner could have would be a Queen, 2 points, or two Jacks, 1 point each. So if West is thinking, he will realize that once he takes his Diamond Ace, South can run nine tricks without the Club finesse. But for the moment West is not quite on top of his game; even so, careful attention to partner's discards will provide the answer and sure defeat.

Now let's take a look at East. His hand doesn't show any sure entries and the contract looks safe to him, so he, too, can be lulled into complacency. But it is a partnership game and you're out to help partner. Therefore when the Diamond King is led you carefully play the 3. You are giving partner a count on the suit; you are telling partner how many Diamonds you have so that if he has the Ace he can control it. (When your hand contains an even number of cards — 2, 4, 6, etc. — you play high-low. When it contains an uneven number — 3, 5, 7, etc. — you play from the bottom up.) So on this hand East plays the 3, starting a high-low count. An alert West holds up the Ace for a further look. If East is playing the 3 from 10-8-3, then declarer has only two Diamonds and West can win the second lead. But if East is discarding, from 3-2, South has three Diamonds and West must hold up till the third round. Easy? Only if you know about it. Only if you take the time to signal. Only if your partner is awaiting your signal. If you're an afternoon player who consistently loses, examine why. Take a look at yourself, your partner, and your opponents. Sure, the game is fun, but maybe you're just playing it for that reason and it's not getting your full attention. But don't be too hard on yourself — remember your reason for playing and enjoy.

This can also work for you when you are playing with someone whose reasons for playing are known to you. During my hunt-and-peck days for a Mixed Pairs partner I continued the social side of life, which inevitably led me to music, which led further to one of the most interesting bridge outings — teaching and playing with a blind musician. When I first met George Shearing, London-born jazz pianist, blind since birth, he was playing only gin. Slowly we added poker to his repertoire and finally bridge.

I had had some experience playing against Dr. Arthur Dye of North Carolina, also blind. Dr. Dye's concentration at the table was astounding, but he was well motivated, so it followed that his game would be good. He used a regular deck of cards whose corners contained the Braille markings. Because these markings raise the height of the cards, they would not fit into the usual duplicate boards. No problem for the good doctor. He brought along his own set of boards to accommodate the Brailled cards, and these would be used throughout his section of play. Dr. Dye would arrange his hand as we did. The only irregularity would occur when the play of the hand started. If Dr. Dye was the declarer, his partner would announce all of his cards as he laid them down. Just as we look at the dummy, Dr. Dye would do it with his fingers. The opponents would announce their cards as they were played. So the blind player records the cards by hearing instead of seeing. With absolute concentration Dr. Dye could play hand after hand without asking you to rename your cards. Or as he gathered in a trick, his fingers would slip over the Braille dots to refresh his memory. He was a good player and did well in many tournaments.

George learned to play, but not well. This had nothing to do with whether he could see or not, but with his reason for playing. It took me a long time to understand this, and I had to conceal my impatience until I did. After a concert I would ask myself how he could play so much music from memory and then sit at the table and ask constantly for a review of the cards. Of course, the answer is quite simple. His reason for playing was to relax completely after he had done his job. He was content with just knowing the game only as a sport, a hobby, between his

sessions of recording, performance, and studying. And so I became a better partner. And so can you. This will bring success
on the scorecard as well as in your head.

Bidding usually brings choices. The best is always to make
the one bid that most accurately describes your hand. The second one is to try to make the one that puts your partner in a
rocking chair. So many times you can make a bid that *you*
understand perfectly but leaves your partner all at sea. Make the
rocking-chair bid and watch your partner relax.

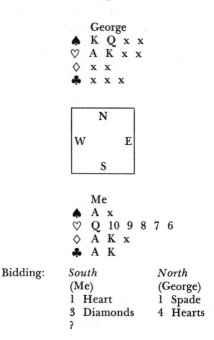

George
♠ K Q x x
♡ A K x x
◇ x x
♣ x x x

Me
♠ A x
♡ Q 10 9 8 7 6
◇ A K x
♣ A K

Bidding:	South	North
	(Me)	*(George)*
	1 Heart	1 Spade
	3 Diamonds	4 Hearts
	?	

The bid that popped into mind was the Grand Slam Force of
5 Notrump. This asks partner to proceed to seven if he holds
two of the top three honors in the trump suit (in this case,

Hearts). I was very comfortable with this bid, but what about my partner? Since he had just played the Mozart K. 459 plus an hour of jazz did I need to foist this on him or was there another way? Look for that other way if it can add an extra bit of insurance to your score. In this case Blackwood would do just fine for us, and Blackwood was something I knew he knew. After 4 Notrump (asking for Aces), if his response to 5 Notrump (asking for Kings) disclosed only one, then we would be safe at 6 Hearts. If, however, his hand held both Kings we could proceed to 7.

The Grand Slam Force is flashy, and in some cases it must be used when you specifically need to know about the trump suit, but this time the rocking-chair bid was available. And as I've said before, if you've really got it together, there's no need at the table to explain to your partner that there is a high-level bid used by experts to cover this situation. You can teach that away from the table at a more propitious moment.

We did have one memorable afternoon of bridge, when George had urged me to point out important mistakes or obvious misplays. As a piano teacher will refrain from nit-picking before a student's performance, so will the bridge instructor refrain from the same when playing a friendly game. In both cases it is best to give just an overall impression. So I very delicately picked on certain points, being careful to choose only the ones that couldn't be discussed at another time. However, it was important to keep his ego in mind. He wanted instruction, yet we were playing with two of his most ardent fans. So how far could I go and how much would he accept? We played very seriously for four hours. I could not measure how far I actually took the helpful hints or how he was accepting them. Unlike Dr. Dye, he was constantly asking us to rename the cards played, including asking the dummy to call his cards again. This is not a criticism, but an indication of the amount of effort he was willing to put into playing. He wasn't exactly lazy, but did only what he felt like doing. This in turn determined the amount of explaining I would do. So when the following hand was dealt I was dealt several choices.

Here is the bidding — and for the moment just look at my hand and the dummy's.

Bidding:	East	South	West	North
	(Me)	(George)	(Fan)	(Fan)
	3 Spades	3 Notrump	Pass	Pass
	Pass			

Opening Lead: 10 of Spades (small cards are incidental)

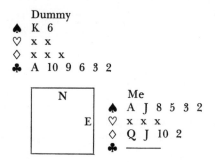

Dummy
♠ K 6
♡ x x
♢ x x x
♣ A 10 9 6 3 2

Me
♠ A J 8 5 3 2
♡ x x x
♢ Q J 10 2
♣ ———

Partner led the Spade 10, George played low, and I went into a think. Certainly he held the Q x x of Spades for his bid. And a further look at the dummy made me quake in my boots when I counted the Club suit — it was certainly going to run for six tricks — and even if he dared take a finesse it would work, as my preemptive bid marked me with short Clubs. So I finally decided that maybe he had a weak link in the Diamond suit. If partner held the Ace we could defeat the hand. So I won the Spade trick with the Ace and shifted to the Diamond. Here's the full deal:

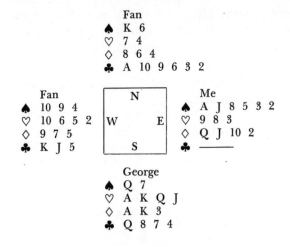

```
                        Fan
                      ♠ K 6
                      ♡ 7 4
                      ◇ 8 6 4
                      ♣ A 10 9 6 3 2

        Fan              N              Me
      ♠ 10 9 4                        ♠ A J 8 5 3 2
      ♡ 10 6 5 2    W         E       ♡ 9 8 3
      ◇ 9 7 5                         ◇ Q J 10 2
      ♣ K J 5            S            ♣ ———

                        George
                      ♠ Q 7
                      ♡ A K Q J
                      ◇ A K 3
                      ♣ Q 8 7 4
```

Obviously my reasoning was right but my play was wrong. George galloped home with eleven tricks.

"How's that?" He glowed.

"Super." I glowered. (Was this the time to mention having stoppers in all four suits for his bid?)

"I think you could have beaten me if you had played the Spade Jack," he suggested.

My ego was definitely on trial. Should I explain why I hadn't? Should I explain that I am an expert? Should I teach on this hand? Will it help anyone? If I was learning anything about myself, now was the time to use it.

"You can make it up to me by playing four hands at the piano when the game is over" — my only answer. At best I can only handle the treble and he could swing all over the bass.

"You're on. In fact, you've been so nice to play with us all afternoon that's the least I can do for you" — his only reply.

As soon as the rubber was over he went to the piano and I went to the bathroom to wash my hands. "What do you want to play?" he called after me.

"How about 'Satin Doll'?" I called back.

And then he sat down and by himself played it better than I have ever heard anyone play it. He really outdid himself. I guess he was playing/saying, "Baby, you may be the Queen of Hearts at the table but at the piano I'm the Ace of Spades, Hearts, Diamonds, and Clubs!" And so it goes.

Another jazz giant, Art Tatum, was a card player. I didn't know him personally, only his music, but I did know Tiny Grimes, guitarist, who played with him many, many times. I was not surprised to learn that Tatum's favorite game was solo. This game is still enjoyed in England and has some of the aspects of bridge. But it is not a partnership game. One bids and plays on his own, and I think this was the appeal for Art Tatum. His work with trios is famous and undeniably great, but he played so much piano one doubted that he ever needed the other players. For many, his solo performances are his best. As in the game of solo, so at the piano he was free to swing, let his mind-boggling improvisations take him to any lengths, unencumbered and not responsible to anyone except himself. Chess players are like this. Some play bridge, just as some bridgers play chess. Both games are great, but the preference for individuality is a strong determining factor.

The bridge circuit offers Individual events from time to time. This is a marvelous challenge to any bridge player. One sits down to play two hands with mostly unknown partners and then on the next round two more hands with another stranger, etc., usually for twenty-eight hands. There is a tremendous element of luck necessary to win with these strangers, whose idiosyncrasies at the table are often funnier than intelligent. I firmly believe that when you play for the first time with anyone it is best to play straight-ahead bridge. Conventions are convenient and fun, but it takes a long time to develop these with regular partners, so with a stranger it could be instant disaster. When faced with a new partner who confronts me with: *"Well,* what do you want to play?" I always answer Blackwood and Stayman. If the player rattles off a long list of conventions I just beg off. So what if you look a little backward. You have just added many points to your score and fewer aspirins to your stomach.

Even expert players using pretty standard conventions can get into mental hassles the first time around. I'll never forget an exchange I overheard between two experts as they boarded a plane for the World Championships in Italy many years ago. They were two of the team's distinguished players, discussing how they played such and such. A third expert turned to me and said, "No wonder we lose. Imagine two people about to play for the championship of the world asking each other such an elementary question on the runway!" And he was right. If they were partners, why hadn't this been settled years ago? It was not a high-level bidding situation, but something as simple as "Do you open five-card majors?"

In Individual events I have encountered players who insist on opening 1 Notrump with 19–21 points, whatever that means, and who make preemptive bids on blank suits, whatever that is supposed to do. How do they think success will find them when on each round they have to explain this to their new partners, and the partners in turn have to remember these strange innovations on an already complicated game?

Keep this in mind the next time you play with the new girl on the block or the new player at your club or the new man in your life; play it close to the chest and easy. Save the intrigue for later and put your partners in that rocking chair.

One of the more deadly Individual events is the one for Life Masters. This accumulation of points places one in bridgedom's Hall of Fame. There was a time when it had real meaning, when one had to play one's guts out to acquire the number of points, 300, to be a Life Master. Competition was fierce for the coveted gold card. But as with everything else commercialism took over, and to insure larger membership (which means more money), players were encouraged to vie for this title via a lesser road. Edgar Kaplan, cofounder of the Kaplan–Sheinwold system and editor of *Bridge World,* found himself seated across the table during a Life Masters' Individual with the proverbial Little Old Lady from Pasadena. They were defending 1 Notrump doubled. Actually, Edgar had doubled and the LOL had passed, showing her willingness to play it there. LOL got off to the wrong opening lead, halfway through the hand she made the wrong switch, and at trick twelve she still could have defeated the hand — but to keep her record clean she didn't. And in keeping with blaming partner, especially when partner is known to be better than you, she leaned across the table and said to Edgar, "I thought to double *you* had to have at least sixteen points!"

"Madam," replied Edgar, "I thought *you* had to have three hundred."

So another chicken hit the dust.

It was time for this chicken to examine her motives vis-à-vis Mixed Pairs partners. If Dr. Dye's and George Shearing's reasons for playing bridge were clear to me, then certainly my own should be explored. My enthusiasm for the game had propelled me into all events, but to sustain it the aforementioned male partners had to be sidelined. It was no longer a matter of just playing to play. To continue in Mixed Pairs events I had to find male partners who appreciated a female who loved the game and a female who would choose her own lovemate away from the table. And when you have dealt with your reasons the sun comes up, your game gets better, and your partners begin to play better with you. And you know exactly why the chicken crossed the road.

12—

Knights in Winning Armor

"HE'S BLACK, isn't he?" asked my roommate.

"I don't know. He didn't ask me if I was Jewish, so I didn't ask him if he was black."

She was referring to my new Mixed Pairs partner, who rode into my life, lasso in hand, and saved me from all the bucking broncos.

Dr. Joseph Henry, tall, handsome, married to an equally lovely lady, Dorothy (not a bridge player). Joe was a practicing dentist as well as a professor at Howard University. I hadn't been out of braces for too long and had four bothersome wisdom teeth, so this gave us something else in common. I don't remember how we found each other, but I presume the law of supply and demand was in effect.

Every time I played in the Washington, D.C., area I would see Dr. Henry and his male partner, also black, playing in the Open events. At the time they were the only Negroes entered. The "why" never occurred to me. What did occur to me was that Joe Henry would be a sensational Mixed Pairs partner. This was reinforced when the following hand took place. I was sitting East and Joe, the Declarer, South.

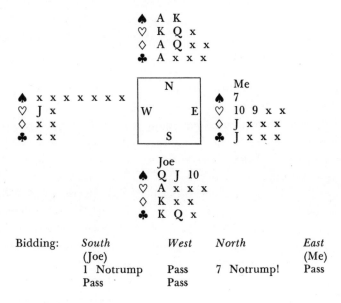

♠ A K
♡ K Q x
◇ A Q x x
♣ A x x x

♠ x x x x x x x		**Me**
♡ J x		♠ 7
◇ x x		♡ 10 9 x x
♣ x x		◇ J x x x
		♣ J x x x

Joe
♠ Q J 10
♡ A x x x
◇ K x x
♣ K Q x

Bidding:	*South*	*West*	*North*	*East*
	(Joe)			(Me)
	1 Notrump	Pass	7 Notrump!	Pass
	Pass	Pass		

Opening Lead: Low Spade

Joe was forced to play the King from the dummy and I was forced (restricted choice!) to play my singleton 7. He then played the Ace from the dummy. I sat rigid — what could I discard?

"I'm squeezed," I looked into his eyes.

"I know," he looked back.

"At trick two!" I exclaimed.

"Does it hurt?" he continued.

"A lot. It's a first for me."

He then cashed the King-Queen of Hearts and then the Ace-King-Queen of Diamonds. I couldn't stand it any longer and just slipped my cards back into the duplicate board. I could have done it immediately, but my partner didn't believe it either. Our rapport as opponents was obvious, and it continued as partners. Although we never discussed the issue of race, we both knew it would never be an issue between us. When Dr. Henry asked me to play in our first Mixed Pairs event I could hardly stop myself from hugging him right on the spot. And when Dorothy asked me to dinner I did hug her on the spot. No more coffee shops with Yankee and no more dining rooms with North #10.

But if one struggle subsided, another soon took its place. The Washington Bridge League became a hotbed of internal struggle when Brigadier General Robert Gill* proposed an amendment to the American Contract Bridge League. This group is the national authority and governing body for all organized bridge activities on the North American continent. If you find yourself playing for master points in East Cupcake, Michigan, you are playing under its aegis. Major cities have individual units, such as the Washington, D.C., Bridge Association, the Richmond Bridge Association, etc., and these in turn form larger units; e.g., the above units are known as the Mid-Atlantic Regional. This procedure is followed throughout the United States. Smaller clubs function within this framework but pay their dues to the parent organization, affectionately called the ACBL. Any club issuing Master Points must be a franchised member of the ACBL or its points aren't worth the pink or white paper they're written on. The whole thing comes off like the head bone's connected to the neck bone, etc.

General Gill's proposed amendment, "that each unit be the sole judge of membership in its territory," was adopted. Both he and the governing body felt that local units would and should know the best way to handle the racial issue. Maybe Memphis or

*General Gill, Baltimore attorney and bridge personality. President ACBL, 1941; Chairman ACBL committee on membership eligibility, 1952.

Richmond or Dallas would be slower in admitting blacks into their memberships, but it never occurred to anyone that Washington, D.C., would be torn apart. Just its name and what it stands for seemed to insure rapid assimilation. Not so. And into this yawning pit fell Joe Henry and I.

As long as the issue had not arisen, the future dissenting Washington members had not raised their ugly heads. "Token blacks," a phrase coined by Lenny Bruce, denoted their acceptance of Joe and his partner. I don't know how they referred to us, but once the infighting started, our hitherto opponents became our archenemies. They would hit me with: "Do you play all the red suits while he plays all the black ones?"

We became a bit "outrageous" — a player's description — when we were seen hugging one another in Richmond after a long absence. As I said, Joe and I were aware of it but we refrained from discussing it. We would arrange our dates, and whatever had to be handled we would handle. We were not a team of ostriches; we just did what we knew had to be done.

But where had all the black players been? In the early days of contract bridge Negroes were excluded from most major tournaments, so a small group of players in the Greater New York area banded together and in 1932 founded the American Bridge Association (ABA). Like the ACBL, the ABA grew and soon divided itself into local and regional units, as well as establishing a master-point system. Naturally, the leading player and highest-ranking one was Dr. Henry.

Until I met Joe Henry I was completely unaware of the ABA and its reason for being. Most of my bridge-playing cronies were just as amazed as I. How could we have been so unthinking? What we were thinking now was, could *we* play there? The ABA welcomed us as cordially as we could have expected, but when the lines were drawn in Washington we became a family of champions, champing at the bit for our championing rights. We were only a handful in those days . . . but you know the end of the story.

In 1964 federal legislation forbade the exclusion of Negroes from hotels, etc., and the ACBL followed speedily with a regulation insuring the right of any ACBL member to play in any National Tournament no matter where it was held. The governing body of and for bridge players has never turned its back on controversial issues. It has acted judiciously at all times, which makes me and its hundreds of thousands of members proud to be members.

Not only was the black issue being put to bed, so was the issue of my Mixed Pairs partners. This chicken not only crossed the road but let every rooster within earshot know why. And as the night followeth the day Joe Henry became my knight. He was daring and frisky at the table — but whoever heard of an undaring knight? His friskiness combined with his daring produced the following results on a hand where we were the defenders.

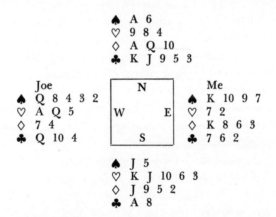

```
                    ♠ A 6
                    ♡ 9 8 4
                    ◇ A Q 10
                    ♣ K J 9 5 3

   Joe                   N              Me
♠ Q 8 4 3 2                          ♠ K 10 9 7
♡ A Q 5            W         E        ♡ 7 2
◇ 7 4                                 ◇ K 8 6 3
♣ Q 10 4                S            ♣ 7 6 2

                    ♠ J 5
                    ♡ K J 10 6 3
                    ◇ J 9 5 2
                    ♣ A 8
```

South bought the hand for 4 Hearts. The opening 7 of Diamonds lead was finessed, so I won the 10 with my King. I returned the 8 of Diamonds, my highest one, thereby requesting a

Spade switch if partner regained the lead. Declarer won this trick in the dummy and led the 9 of Hearts, playing low from his hand while frisky Joe daringly played the Ace! Joe returned a Spade as I had requested, declarer winning the return with the Ace in the dummy. Declarer believes he is home free, for surely I have the Heart Queen. Declarer can now count ten tricks with the finesse (Queen of trumps) working, but he shouldn't have counted Joe Henry out. Confidently declarer took the Heart finesse, Joe gobbled it up with the Queen, played a Spade to my King, and then ruffed the Diamond return with his last trump. If Joe had won the first trump finesse with the Queen, declarer would have been forced into the alternate line of play — the Club finesse for the Queen — which would have worked and provided him with a parking place for his losing Spade.

The Diamond 8 returned by me at trick two is known as a suit-preference play. A high card asks for the highest of the remaining obvious suits and a low card asks for the lower of the two remaining suits. In this case Spades were high and Clubs were low (Hearts being the trump suit). Even if the suit-card preferences are as low as the 3 and 2, the 3 becomes the highest card and the 2 the lowest. Partner must pay close attention to the spots to determine when a 3 is high. Sometimes the Gods (or now the computers) do not deal you the exact spots you'd like.

This brings to mind one of the all-time super cheating stories, which became a legend. Mr. X's partner led the Ace of a suit. Mr. X did not want the suit continued, but upon close examination of his cards found only the 8 and 9 in his hand. Either one would ask for the continuation. Mr. X dropped the 8 on the floor, and as he leaned down to pick it up said, "Low card coming!" This *irregularity* was promptly dealt with by the directors.

The world of bridge took on a new glow for me when I was partnered by Joe, and the glow deepened when Sidney Silodor asked me to play with him in a Mixed Teams event in New York

City. Some experts when playing with lesser players scream, some twist their hair, some drink, some sulk, some disappear forever, but Sidney made the game totally enjoyable. From the lesser player's point of view, if you're smart you'll relax in the comforting knowledge that your every play and bid will be caught by expert hands. You can also relax when you are the dummy, for again the cards are in capable hands. And finally, when you are defending, it is heaven to know your partner is watching and awaiting your every move. The expert who can bring this off with his partner is assured of getting his partner's best game.

The suit-preference signaling described above is known in England as the "McKenney," in recognition of one of its pioneers. The inventor, Hy Lavinthal, brought this handy tool into bridge parlance in 1933. And in the following hand Sidney made it double-or-nothing "McKenney."

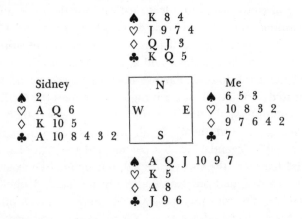

```
                    ♠ K 8 4
                    ♡ J 9 7 4
                    ◇ Q J 3
                    ♣ K Q 5

    Sidney              N              Me
♠ 2                                ♠ 6 5 3
♡ A Q 6          W         E        ♡ 10 8 3 2
◇ K 10 5                            ◇ 9 7 6 4 2
♣ A 10 8 4 3 2          S          ♣ 7

                    ♠ A Q J 10 9 7
                    ♡ K 5
                    ◇ A 8
                    ♣ J 9 6
```

South was the declarer at 4 Spades. Sidney led the Ace of Clubs, the suit he had bid. I dropped the 7. Sidney continued the suit with the 10 — suit preference, or Pat, this is how you can get back to me for another ruff. So I dutifully and gratefully returned the 2 of Hearts. South played low and Sidney won with the Queen. He then led the 2 of Clubs and again I trumped — and returned another Heart, for I knew Sidney had the Ace. Declarer went down two tricks.

When the opponents left the table (and not one minute before) Sidney calmly said, "Pat, I *commanded* you to return a Diamond. For the Diamond return defeats the contract another trick." (In tournament play this additional trick could be the difference between winning and losing.) He did not yell or scream or embarrass me; he said (and it is worth repeating), "I commanded you . . ." And that's what playing with an expert like Sidney Silodor was all about.

I had been lulled into complacency, knowing the location of the Heart Ace, and let up. His original play of the Club 10 was correct and so was I in returning the low Heart. His play of the Club 2 was just as correct. It was the second suit-preference signal — for a Diamond, not a Heart. He reasoned that my Heart 2 could be from four, which left declarer with only the King; therefore it was necessary to establish his Diamond King before the Heart Ace was gone. Once the Heart Ace was cleared, dummy's Jack of Hearts was established for a discard of declarer's losing Diamond. So here was McKenney twice in one hand. A very good lesson for me and one for the future, when I became more expert, in handling partners.

Sidney's death in 1963 left a huge void in the lives of all who knew him, and Joe Henry — well, he's a full professor at the Harvard School of Dental Medicine. But when Joe gave up bridge, he left it with flying colors. In an effort to promote his system, C. C. Wei* toured the country, challenging local teams. Joe Henry and his teammates met the challenge in Washington, D.C. It was played before an audience of more than three hundred at the Sheraton Park Hotel, with columnist and author Fred

---

* See C. C. Wei, *Precision Simplified* (New York: Monna Lisa Precision Pub., 1972); Charles H. Goren, *Charles H. Goren Presents the Precision System* (New York: Doubleday, 1971).

Karpin as moderator. The Precision team offered $1,000 to any team who could beat them, and that's exactly what Joe Henry and his team did. Throughout the tour the Henry team remained the only victorious one, which says a lot for it — and a lot for the Precision team and system, too.

Dr. Henry to the end remained the frisky and daring player I've described, but when it was time to be disciplined he was that, too. One day I confronted him with an opening bid of 5 Spades (no need to make a rocking-chair bid with Joe). He knew I was asking specifically about the trump suit: Bid 6 Spades if you hold the Ace or King, 7 Spades if you hold both. Joe gazed at his hand in almost total disbelief:

> Spades: x
> Hearts: A K x x
> Diamonds: A K J x x
> Clubs: x x x

He was probably wondering how I could make such a bid when he held two Aces and two Kings. But he was disciplined and trusting; he passed. Would you have? My hand:

> Spades: Q J 10 9 8 7 6 5 4 3
> Clubs: A K Q

Bridge partnerships, like life partnerships, require trust, daring, discipline, and the ability to hold your tongue at the right time.

13—

Three Jacks and a Queen

WHEN YOUR REASONS for doing something become clear to all around you, they in turn follow suit. It just takes a while for the dust to settle and the smog to lift. If you're a free-lance tennis buff looking for the right partner, eventually you'll be found or you'll do the finding. If you're a serious player you'll end up with a serious partner, or vice versa. That stinking old adage about water and its level is quite true. But before you plummet into your niche, apprenticeship is important, paying your dues a must.

A young musician was telling George Shearing one day, "If only I could have one big record — one shot on the Carson show — then I'd have it made."

George smiled. "Maybe you're right, but it won't last unless you've done your homework. And in our business, homework means playing the rinky-dink towns, bastard pianos, one-nighters — there is no short cut to success."

And he's right. For if we take the short cut we're not ready for the big time. When the three Jacks, all named Dick, came bounding into my bridge life I was indeed ready. They brought with them the "balance" so necessary in a bridge player's life. But without the years of apprenticeship I would not have been ready. I'd fought off the ego madmen who bid Notrump ad infinitum, come to grips with the male players who played for fun waiting for the postgame "fun," and discarded the tons of others who made the game intolerable. I'd learned to deal with my spouse, boyfriend, or lover and his reasons for doing what and why at the table, making the best of it with understanding, tolerance, and the desire to play with *him*.

Balance in anything is important. If partner makes a misstep and you can correct it, do just that. Put your partnership back in balance. Who knows, you may need it next time around. In bridge the basic balance technique applies when the person to your left opens the bidding and the next two players pass. You are now in what we call the "pass out" position and must carefully consider your hand before you willy-nilly let the bidding die. Obviously the partner of the opening bidder has less than 6 points or he would have responded. You know what to do with a big hand, but what about with weaker ones?

With a scattering of points, plus the points partner figures to have, it behooves you to bid. Partner needs your protection — he has failed to bid for a reason and you are there to bring about balance. How to reopen calls for good judgment, acquired by doing it over and over again — not just a one-shot with Goren or Carson.

With a balanced hand and something in the opening bidder's suit, you can protect with 1 Notrump. This is not the same as an opening bid of 1 Notrump. With a suit of your own and a scattering of points, but slightly unbalanced, bid your suit. With a good hand and a willingness to play in partner's suit or defend, then reopen with a double. This gives partner the option of passing for penalties if he has made a trap pass. But don't sell out any more than you would fail to take a swing at the tennis ball if it fell at your feet after partner had missed it. You will find that if you bid, part-scores will show up on your side of the tally more often than on the side of your opponents.

For example:	*South*	*West*	*North*	*East*
	(Dealer)			(You)
	1 Heart	Pass	Pass	?

Your hand:	Spades: A Q x x x
	Hearts: x
	Diamonds: x x x
	Clubs: J x x x

This is a typical balance position. You are bidding your hand plus partner's, so protect by bidding 1 Spade.

Now let's turn to the person being protected, your partner. A good one will not, should not, punish you for being aware. If the opening bidder passes then partner should be careful if he decides to bid. In other words, if you have gone out on a limb to protect the combined hands, he mustn't hang you on the limb.

Let's return to the hand. You've balanced with 1 Spade and partner holds:

> Spades: K J x x
> Hearts: A Q x x
> Diamonds: x
> Clubs: K x x x

This is a good hand, but any bid over 1 Heart was uncomfortable. Partner could not:

1. double for business or take-out.
2. overcall on a four-card suit.
3. bid a misleading Notrump.

Partner did the right thing by passing, knowing you would balance. The second right thing for partner to do is to bid only

3 Spades, not 4. The bid of 4 is the "hanging bid" while the bid of 3 allows some leeway, in case your balance is weak. A good partner will protect your protection.

This is a very delicate business. Jack Number 1 was explaining it very carefully before our first game together. So I promised to love, honor, and protect. The bidding went as follows:

South	East	North	West
	(Me)		(Jack No. 1)
1 Heart	Pass	1 Notrump	Pass
Pass	???		

Here I was in the pass-out position holding 10 very nice points. I protected with a very nice Double. Jack dutifully responded with his best suit and the next voice we heard was North, the weak responder, saying "Double." Oh well, I thought, just bid your best suit, but again the opponent doubled. Jack-be-nimble tried a third suit and North's "Double" came out before Jack had finished the last sound. No matter where we tried to land (looking for our best spot, known as scrambling), good old North was there with a Double. I wasn't sure balancing had so much going for it as I initialed the score, down 700. Reading my mind, Jack asked me to look at North's hand. North had meant to bid 2 Notrump, slightly larger than 1 Notrump — no, a lot larger. So we got caught in the net of his mistake. But the beauty of Jack or any good partner is that neither will criticize you for doing the right thing, even when it boomerangs to the tune of 700 points. Never. Balancing and protection will pay off for you over and over again. Use it more carefully when playing straight rubber bridge, but in duplicate or Chicago weigh in. The higher the level the better your hand must be to balance, but always be on the alert before you simply pass — the hand might just belong to you.

Perhaps many of the husband-wife or male-female skirmishes

stem from a lack of understanding about balance. The male player, usually more aggressive, will duck in and out of the bidding because he feels his female partner is too timid. The female (who when she is aggressive will outdistance the male every time) knows this about her partner, but can't read his sound bids from his unsound ones. She is off balance. You must put your house in order. If you and your partner do not employ the protection bid, discuss it and put it in your bidding house tonight. Assure your partner he or she will not have to make miscalls out of fear. For fear not, you will protect.

Jack Number 2 picked up where Jack Number 1 had left off in the bridge education of Pat. All three of these men were good players who enjoyed female company. The so-called female approach to bridge might have caused them to wince occasionally but it did not go either unnoticed or unappreciated. After all it was the men who gave us the female intuition label — wasn't it? So if they didn't understand it they shouldn't have started it in the first place. But my three Jacks were secure enough to play Mixed Pairs events, secure enough to let me play Notrumps, and had a healthy respect for any player trying to improve. This new-found secure male encouraged me to slip him a Notrump or two and to stop jockeying for position. All of which adds up to more time to spend on the important elements of the game. Jack Number 2 introduced me to another kind of Notrump protection: the unusual balancing act at the 2 level. Once you've secured the hatches at the 1 level proceed to the next. Selling out at higher levels can be just as disastrous to your score as at lower ones.

Bidding:	South	East	North	West
	(Dealer)	(Jack No. 2)		(Me)
	1 Heart	Pass	2 Hearts	Pass
	Pass	2 Notrump	Pass	???

Jack had flipped his flipper. How could he come into the bidding at the 2 level when he had failed to take action earlier? Unusual. In any language very unusual. But he was a good player, not frivolous, not a showoff. When you find yourself playing with this kind of partner, do your best to determine what could be going on in his head. Don't write him off as a fruitcake.

"Alvin Roth devised this bid many years ago," he told me. "When you have a two-suiter [at least five cards in two suits] and not enough points to make a take-out double, you show it by bidding Two Notrump. This is easily recognized because the real Two Notrump bid would call for first a double followed by a bid. Certainly a passed hand must be making an unusual bid." My hand:

Spades: A x x x
Hearts: K x x x
Diamonds: Q 10 x
Clubs: x x

We were playing the Unusual Notrump just for minor suits. (Some players have refined this and play it for the unbid major and a minor suit. I have always kept to just minors and aggressively bid my major suits. It's a matter of preference.) With the above hand I bid 3 Diamonds after Jack bid 2 Notrump. He had not doubled; therefore he was not interested in my four-card Spade suit. You must trust your partner and bid your best minor, knowing your partner has at least five in that suit. Now when I say I was finally ready for the three Jacks it is understandable. Can you imagine Yankee or the others making this bid or, worse yet, my trusting them? As your game develops along with partnership understanding and trust, your enjoyment increases beyond your wildest expectations. It's safe to say the game takes on another dimension. And I hope this is what this book is all about.

"And what is an Alvin Roth?" I asked from the new bridge cloud on which I was balancing.

"An Alvin Roth is a man with a mind that invents right at the card table, at the dinner table, in the bathtub — wherever the Roth mind happens to be," he replied.

"I've got to meet an Alvin Roth."

The following week Jack Number 3 and I were playing in the National Charity game. Each year the ACBL designates a charity, and the tournament receipts from the entire country are turned over to it.

The gentleman at the table was playing with his wife. There was nothing unusual about this. What was unusual was her bidding. She bid only Clubs — no matter what cards she held. It was funnier than confusing. Furthermore, they always landed in the right contract with the man playing it. As we walked away from the table, Jack said, "That was Alvin Roth."

"And that was his programmed wife, plugged into Clubs?"

"Right. But there's an explanation."

"I certainly hope so."

Jack continued, "Well, she plays very little bridge, so Alvin agreed to play with her in the Charity game only if she agreed to bid just Clubs. That was two years ago, and they won. Last year he allowed her to add Diamonds to her bidding but they finished a measly second. So this year she's back to just Clubs."

And they won!

Alvin Roth has a magic mind. It is a nonstop express to every village, city, and country of bridge thought. His famous system,* written in collaboration with Tobias Stone, is played and enjoyed by many of the bridge greats. The winning record compiled by Roth-Stoners in national play in 1952 is still unbelievable.

Mr. Roth lived in Washington, D.C., at that time, which enabled all of us to become his disciples — the three Jacks, Terry and Mike Michaels, Said and Betty Haddad, and scores of others.

---

* The Roth-Stone System: *Al Roth on Bridge* (Washington, D.C.: Melville Publishers, 1953).

We sat at his feet, sat behind him when he played, listened to him after every session or whenever the famous Roth mouth opened. He became our guru. The light from this bridge star led us down the path of better bridge and greater victories.

"What's it like to play with him?" I asked Betty Haddad one day as she emerged from a four-hour session partnered by him.

"He does manage to keep you a bit off balance. Not because he isn't great — but because he is so great you want to do everything right."

"I see what you mean. That's a bit unbalancing." I sympathized.

"For example," she continued, "I held this hand as dealer."

> Spades: x
> Hearts: A K x x x
> Diamonds: A K x x x x
> Clubs: x

"Playing with you, Pat, I would know exactly what to open and rebid. But with Alvin my head went like this: Should I open Hearts and then bid Diamonds or should I open Diamonds and then bid Hearts or should I bid Hearts, then Diamonds-Diamonds or bid Diamonds, then Hearts-Hearts . . ."

"So what did you do?"

"I just said the hell with it and passed."

"Oh, my God" was all I could say. "What did he do?"

"Well, he opened with Hearts and thought I had lost all my marbles when as a passed hand I pushed him into slam."

"In Hearts or Diamonds?" Trying to make her feel better.

But you see, there is no way we could ever have explained to him the effect he had on us at the table. So we learned from him, tried desperately to get it all together when we played with him, accepted the fact that when we were his opponents he could see right through the backs of our cards, and prayed a lot. Alvin never really understood why we came apart at the seams; he just went on winning and winning and inventing and inventing no matter who became his partner.

I had a similar experience with him in a team game in New York many years later. He opened the bidding with 1 Diamond, I bid 1 Heart, and he bid 1 Notrump. My hand:

> Spades: A x x x
> Hearts: K x x x
> Diamonds: J x x x
> Clubs: x

Do you believe I passed? I don't believe it either. I remember looking at him, thinking about Betty, and bursting out laughing. The opponents were so befuddled when they saw the dummy, they forgot to take their first six Club tricks. I found Betty in the hall and told her the story, which didn't amaze her. Her only response was: "I told you he's marvelous. Anyone else would have gone down."

And that was the spell of Alvin Roth on us. *The Official Encyclopedia of Bridge* spells it out this way: "Roth, Alvin, one of the great players of all time, generally considered the most original bidding theorist of his bridge generation."

The three Jacks and I, armed with Roth-Stone, took off for Canada and the Canadian Championships. The room clerk gave us the north-of-the-border fisheye when we requested only two rooms. But we got his eye off the hook as we explained, one room with three beds and one with one bed. Two Jacks entered the Men's Pairs, the third directed the action, and I kibitzed two of the local stars. Jack the director had pointed out to me many years ago, "It is always a good idea to watch your future opponents in action from the sidelines. Then when you come up against them you are better prepared." This is a good rule to follow if you have a five- or six-handed game at home. Instead of wandering to the pantry when you are the out player, pull up a chair and watch. In picking up some of their bridgeisms you'll be a better partner and bitter opponent.

I was watching Eric Murray and Sammy Kehela, Canada's All-Stars, when Jack Number 1 limped by, assisted by two directors.

"Food poisoning," one director said.

"Don't believe it." Jack managed a weak smile. "It's their constant overcalling on four-card Spade suits — turns my stomach." He made a fast exit and never returned.

The director returned and quite apologetically asked if I would fill in. "In a Men's Pairs?" squeaked barrister Murray.

"In our Men's Pairs?" squawked Sammy Kehela.

"I'm afraid so," squirmed the director.

"Love to," squealed I.

As I was seated across the table from Jack Number 2, the fun fur began to fly and fly and fly. The procession of males partnered by males continued all afternoon. By the time most of them reached our table, word had already reached them that a woman was sitting in — in their inner sanctum.

Well, girls, they're not so different from us. If you play in a regular game with your female friends, you certainly are aware of which one is aggressive Annie — her cakes will rise even when she's forgotten the baking powder. If it's passive Patsy, she'll cook on a bonfire when her oven is on the fritz. Well, don't they behave the same way at the table? So do the boys; it's only a matter of getting to know them. If Myrtle's husband makes a play for you at a Saturday night dance he'll make the same play for you at the table.

I began to compartmentalize them mentally and plan my strategy accordingly.

1. The twins. These tight-lipped, slightly scrawny, medium-priced suiters have been loyal employees for years. They will

make the same tight-lipped, correctly learned, scrawny bids against you. Each is true to his bid, loyal to his partner, and of course cut from the same medium-priced cloth. Hardly ever will they have a big game, but they will grace the middle of the road like the double-white-line type of players they really are. Be careful playing against them, but you can cross over the line even with another bid coming; the twins will slow down for you. As the sun will rise and set, they will pay their taxes before the fifteenth and always have their bids.

2. The salesmen. These guys have a bag full of tricks. Just when you think they are about to walk out the front door, they turn around with just one more pitch. Similarly at the table, when you think the bidding is over, back they come for one more crack at you. Don't fall into their trap. Not vulnerable, double them, or if they're vulnerable, pass and take your sure profit. Next time out they may have switched brands, but their sales pitch is the same.

3. Happy-go-lucky Charlies. They're just playing for the fun of it . . . so they say. But their passes at their secretaries were on the level and so were their failures to score. This kind scares me to death. Sometimes they're on the level and sometimes they're not. They are to be feared like the love-ins (Chapter 9) for different reasons. Under the guise of the original Ha-Ha boys, they make semisound bids, play semisound defense, and would take a semipeek at your hand while giving you a semipeck on the cheek. Someone up there is trying to help them, but instead of listening, they are waiting to tell the latest Farmer's Daughter joke. Keep your eyes on your cards; if they ask for the time, tell them your watch is broken. Try to do the normal thing and thank God when they leave — it's always hard to get them to do so.

4. Married-forever Sams. These are the Martyred Boys sans Sunshine. They are fairly reliable but not very inventive. Just as they yearn for one last fling but wouldn't take it, so they long

for one more bid, which they won't make. On the golf course these are the guys who make a hole-in-one, are awarded a year's supply of baby food — only it happens when their kids are in college. You hate to punish them as they're so damned nice, but on the other hand, would you have an affair with them out of pity?

5. The young smart alecks. You wish you could teach them a lesson, but they have just enough going for them to make you uneasy. They've studied the game, studied you, studied their partners, their parents, and the parents of their partners while trying to bury you with their studied intense looks. Remember you've been around longer, theirs is mostly façade, so try to let them hang themselves. Maybe with their own hair.

6. The expert pairs. They will not cheat against you. Some may keep you slightly off balance — you know, glance at another blonde while making love to you over a bottle of Chablis. Just be smart. Learn from them, play slowly (as you would sip that Chablis), pick their brains not their pockets, and don't do anything out of the ordinary (like flirting with the brunet jock at the next table). Remember they are disciplined, courageous, battle-scarred, and out to win. If your side gets to game and makes it, you have won the Croix de Guerre. Don't take any flyers — for sure, they'll clip your wings.

7. Ex-husbands–ex-lovers. If you can remember why they are "exes" you've got it made. If he was cheating on you, he'll be apt to try it at the table. Call the director. If he constantly picked on you and put you down, turn-about is fair play. Watch for the moment to set him and do it. Don't let him trap you into one more dangerous bid ("Let's try one more time; I'll change") and put you down again. Fool me once, shame on you; fool me twice, shame on me. You know what makes this Tom, Dick, or Harry run. If you don't come out on top then you need a re-fresher course.

8. The also-rans. There are always several horses that make up the field. When you've played against them often enough you can clock them and compile your own track record and past performance chart. Once in a while at 99–1 they'll score, so next time watch them carefully. If they're playing badly they will try to come from behind. Let them go to the outside while you continue to hug the rail. Their jockey partners are not the best, so straight ahead for you while they take to the whip.

I loved playing in the Men's Pairs in Canada. I loved all the male opponents and especially Jack, my partner, who unlike his one-eyed brothers played as if he had three — one in the back of his head.

Did we win? Only my bridge-playing male hairdresser knows for sure.

14—

"Oscar"

For years we've all sat around watching the stars clasp their Oscars and thank anyone whose name they can remember. Well, in St. Louis, with the National Women's Team Trophy clasped firmly in my hand, that's what I wanted to do. Jacks Numbers 1, 2, and 3 were there cheering, as well as Sidney Silodor and Alvin Roth. Teammates, Terry Michaels and I had not only won the title but had become eligible for the first Women's Olympic Bridge Team. Only sixteen U.S. ladies qualified for this honor, and our team comprised six of the sixteen.

Sterling silver bridge trophies have different values at different times. The nicely shaped ones became interesting vegetable servers. My son would always scrape the bottom and announce with great glee: "This one is from the Northern Virginia Bridge Championship, Women's Pairs," or as he swiftly removed the last vestige of spinach: "This is from the Mixed Pairs Mid-Atlantic Regional." It was always a game to see if we could remember which one was from which tournament before we reached the bottom. He never quite caught on to my ruse of getting him to

eat his vegetables. Any more than he understands why I would
never hock the first one I won when he was still in my stomach.
And therein lies another use for the sterling. When you fall on
bad times they are easily replaced with money. Somewhere, perhaps, another tiny tot is scraping the bottom and wondering what
the devil a Hearst Team of Four is!

But for the moment the St. Louis prize was all mine, and as I
reached home with it my son announced it was worth a Grand
Marnier soufflé, not the Birdseye special of the week.

The trials for the Olympic Team were held in Miami seven
months after the St. Louis victory. The hotel was agog with
players, staff, and reporters. One of the women finalists asked if
I intended to stay and play after the trials ended. A casual
"Why?" from me was answered with just as casual a response: "A
friend of mine is looking for a partner to play the Mixed Pairs
event." This lady player being Jan Stone, the distaff side of
the Stone in Roth-Stone, she was not about to fix me up with a
jerk, so again I casually asked, "Who?"

"Alfred Sheinwold" was her reply.

We became a love-in couple, who became engaged, who subsequently married. Love-in means never having to say you're
sorry 'cause you never blow a hand. If you're searching for an
elusive Queen, the opponent drops it on the table while reaching
for a cigarette. Love-in means all suits break 3-3 and all Kings
are onside. Love-in means when you open the bidding out of
turn, your right-hand opponent screams, *"Director."* And . . .

"Ms. Love-in," he says almost apologetically, "you may make
any bid you like, but Mr. Love-in is barred from the whole
bidding auction."

Now it's your turn to do something. Your bid, in this case my
bid of 1 Notrump, can stand or can be changed. Either way
partner must pass throughout the bidding, so you've not a clue as
to the value of his cards — and partner is not allowed to suggest,

wiggle, look at the sky, or hum. But fear not when you are a love-in, help is on its way.

There he sat, my Mr. Love-in, so trusting, not a cross wrinkle on his brow. I wanted to make such a good impression. How to do it with *crème d'humiliation* splattered all over my face. Never underrate Cupid. He flew over my head whispering sweet nothing Notrumps in my ear and out it came: "Three Notrump." Everyone else passed.

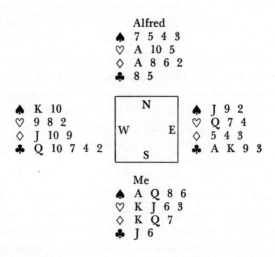

Alfred
♠ 7 5 4 3
♡ A 10 5
◇ A 8 6 2
♣ 8 5

♠ K 10
♡ 9 8 2
◇ J 10 9
♣ Q 10 7 4 2

♠ J 9 2
♡ Q 7 4
◇ 5 4 3
♣ A K 9 3

Me
♠ A Q 8 6
♡ K J 6 3
◇ K Q 7
♣ J 6

West gets off to his best lead, a small Club. You play low from the dummy, East plays his Ace, you follow (wondering how to explain this to your love), as East returns a low Club. He is hoping to put you to the guess — he assumes his partner holds the Jack because you certainly hold the Queen for your bid. You play your Jack and West wins with the Queen. Now West switches to a Diamond because you must have the King of Clubs for your bid (see how confusing, but not inaccurate). You proceed to take the rest of the tricks, finessing for the Heart Queen the right way — you know where the King of Clubs is and you're not about to let *that* opponent in, especially because he's the one who broke the spell and screamed *"Director."* Thus making 3 Notrump while those around you are going down, even if they are in 4 Spades. And arm in arm you walk away, leaving the debris all over the floor. You head for the champagne fountain, which no one could ever convince you is just an old, enameled water cooler.

In Chapter 9 I have already described another Alfred-Pat near–love-in disaster. But here is my favorite.

Sonny Moyse, former editor and publisher of *Bridge World* magazine, was famous for his articles about the games he played with his wife, Jackie. He called her Angel to the end — one of bridgedom's true love-ins.

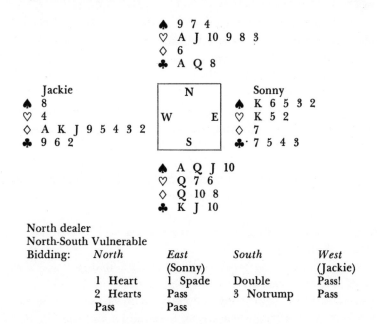

♠	9 7 4	
♡	A J 10 9 8 3	
◇	6	
♣	A Q 8	

Jackie
♠ 8
♡ 4
◇ A K J 9 5 4 3 2
♣ 9 6 2

Sonny
♠ K 6 5 3 2
♡ K 5 2
◇ 7
♣ 7 5 4 3

♠ A Q J 10
♡ Q 7 6
◇ Q 10 8
♣ K J 10

North dealer
North-South Vulnerable

Bidding:

North	East	South	West
	(Sonny)		(Jackie)
1 Heart	1 Spade	Double	Pass!
2 Hearts	Pass	3 Notrump	Pass
Pass	Pass		

Sonny dismisses his more than dubious Spade overcall with:

"Well, I was playing with my wife," and tells us that "Jackie always had such faith in my bids that even with a singleton she'd never rescue me." To prove her undying devotion to him, she led her singleton Spade. Her devotion seems more in favor of the opponents, but remember, they were love-ins. The declarer won the lead as Sonny ducked with his King. Declarer was, of course, worried about the Diamond suit, but had no choice, so took the Heart finesse. Sonny, hoping for maybe one or two tricks in Diamonds, switched to his singleton 7. And Jackie cashed Diamonds and Diamonds and Diamonds for down five.

The love-in syndrome is only temporary, but if you're lucky, bridge togetherness can go on indefinitely. Alfred and I knew our reasons for playing the game; re-examine yours. If your turmoils at the table are hectic, go out to dinner with your love and over a bottle of wine discuss your reasons for playing. Whenever one half of a mixed team runs to me with a problem, my friendly bit of advice is: "I think you should be telling him [or her], not me." For it makes little difference if I understand the player's feelings and all the difference in the world if his partner does. All relationships need redefining from time to time. And after the wine takes hold, maybe you could make a few resolutions/ suggestions to your partner, such as:

1. Let's confine our table conversation to compliments only.

2. Any instruction or criticism can only be made after we are home and *in bed*.

3. No more talking behind each other's back — only face-to-face confrontations.

4. No matter how many errors are committed, we will continue to trust each other on subsequent hands.

5. Our system will be understood by both of us, not just one. We both have the right to accept or reject any convention.

6. We appreciate the fact that bridge is a complicated game

and will honor partner's right to make complicated decisions, even if sometimes they are not winning ones.

7. Coffee-housing* will be limited to coffee being served in the house.

This last rule runs rampantly amuck in social rubber games. You probably are aware of it when it happens to you and resent it, but never do anything about it. Or if you are guilty, I hope you are not aware of your unintentional passage of information. There is a big difference between *"I bid* One Spade" and a simple "One Spade." There is never an excuse for folding your cards after a bid. This implies, "That's the end. I have no more to say, so partner, shut up." There is no justification for allegro, then lento, in the music of your voice. Set your own metronome and stick to it.

Charlie Goren was once partnered with a Little Old Lady who passed rather reluctantly over his first Club bid. The second time around she made an even more reluctant pass over his second Club bid. Goren ended up as the declarer in 3 Clubs only to find the lady's hand contained no trick value whatsoever. Quipped the famous Mr. G., "My, that second hesitation certainly was an overbid."

In an effort to cut down on specific communications between partners, the ACBL set in motion a rule to be followed before a preemptive bid. In order for the opponents to be on the alert, the player making the bid must announce his intention of "skipping." For example, if your right-hand opponent is about to open the bidding with 3 Clubs, he should announce: "I am about to make a skip bid." The ACBL ruling calls for you, the next bidder, to wait ten seconds before either bidding or passing. It is a good rule. If you have not been forewarned and hold a

---

* Unethical actions, usually by means of conversation, to relay information to partner or mislead opponents.

smattering of points, you need time to think. The fact that you are thinking tips off your partner. So if you decide to pass, your partner may have the same problem but has been aided by your unintentional slow pass. Partner may now find his way into the bidding — aided and abetted by you. However, having been alerted by the about-to-be skipper, you now have time to make your decision. After ten seconds you bid in tempo. Partner no longer has that extra bit of information.

I was in Atlantic City playing with Martin Cohn of Detroit when the ACBL painstakingly announced this rule. Martin was known for his rather unusual preempts — a blank suit. So after the directors went through the new "alert" the bidding commenced.

MARTIN: I am about to make a skip bid. Three Hearts.

LADY: Mr. Cohn, I am going to wait ten seconds and then double the hell out of you.

It's still a good rule.

Card-playing in European coffee houses may be the original culprit of the coffee-housing actions, or maybe it's the Lower East Side coffee houses of New York. We award them a zero for introducing this into the game but a score of 100 for the hilarious tales derived from it. Groucho Marx, when playing in a game chocked-full-of nut coffee-housers, told his partner, "If you like my lead don't bother to signal with a high card, just smile and nod your head."

The language of bridge is confined to only fifteen words out of the more than 400,000 basic English words:

1. One	5. Five
2. Two	6. Six
3. Three	7. Seven
4. Four	8. Spades

9. Hearts   13. Pass

10. Diamonds   14. Double

11. Clubs   15. Redouble

12. Notrump

The bridge player must use these fifteen words to describe each of the 635,013,559,600 different hands. No wonder we are tempted to add "I" when we bid or pass. Just our voice ego wants to be heard. Have you ever played a game where just the fifteen words were used? We are just not that disciplined. "I" begat "You did." "I did" begat "Okay, then I will." They all begat the opponents into action, which must have begat coffee-housing. So coffee-housing has got to go, and you are the ones to arrange its demise. Can you imagine yourself starting a conversation with a golfer as he is about to take a swing at the ball? Horrors, you say; well, horrors to the players who use the same gamemanship at the bridge table.

So now you are on your second bottle of wine as you and your loved one are rearranging your bridge togetherness. When all your resolutions fail, have an escape clause. TM (transcendental meditation) has introduced mantras — your own magic word for relief of tensions as you put yourself under. Find a mutual mantra for the table. If partner's tone is getting out of hand, use your mutual mantra to stop the action. Just agree on a word, then agree to stop whatever you are doing once either one of you utters it. Most couples have their own language anyhow, so pick one of your love words. "Pecan Pie" always works for me. One couple uses "Shalom," another "Bateau Smooch" (apologies to Mouches), and another just simply gets up and kisses each other. It's foolproof.

When we were not at the card table the Moon over Miami was working overtime on us. When Alfred said, "Will you?" I almost drowned him in the Americana swimming pool with my "Yes." Alan Truscott, bridge writer for the *New York Times,* was helping the moon along with his renditions of British ballads, singing them in the pool. Alan and Alfred are both British, bridge players, writers, singers. Remembering this, I think of us as a foursome: Alfred, Alan, me, and the moon . . . quite a Mixed Team.

I called my son, John, to tell him the happy news.

"Did you win another Oscar?" he asked.

"No, I won an Alfred."

"What's an Alfred?" asked my then twelve-year-old.

"An Alfred loves little boys, shaggy dogs, and horses," I told him.

"Well, we have two out of three," remarked a somewhat puzzled John.

For you see, the first and last requisite for bridge togetherness is humor. Maybe it is also the first and last for a good partnership in anything, and I hit the jackpot with Alfred.

"How did he propose?" asked my son. He assumed he was a bridge player.

"He told me a story." It went like this . . .

"Did you hear about the horse who entered a bridge tournament?"

"No, just the Kentucky Derby."

"Well," continued Alfred, "he bid so well that he and his partner reached a grand slam on the first hand. The horse was the declarer but went down one. His partner reprimanded him by pointing out he, the horse, failed to take the finesse for the King of Clubs.

" 'That's ridiculous,' said the horse. 'Whoever heard of a horse knowing how to finesse?' "

"Hmm," said my son, "Alfreds are as sterling as Oscars."

15—

Forever South

My mother thinks we were married between Thanksgiving and New Year's. We think we were married after the Fall Nationals and before the Spring Nationals. All three of us are correct; it's just a matter of how you look at life.

"So," my mother continued, "you've finally managed to sit South in Alfred's column." I never knew my mother had such an adroit sense of humor. Again she was correct. No matter where we played bridge, I was going to be the proverbial South. Inasmuch as I had abandoned "facing City Hall to finesse" in Chapter 3, it didn't matter which way South faced. There was one problem. If you and your partner have a dispute and one of you says, "Okay, I'll write Sheinwold," you are free to write Sheinwold. But when Sheinwold is your partner and there's a dispute — plus you are a Sheinwold — to whom do you write? Minnie from the old days might have had a solution, but I was thirteen years and thirty-two hundred miles away from her. I'd have to work it out myself.

We lost no time in buying a swimming pool with a house.

Both of us had had enough of cold eastern weather, antifreeze, and snow boots. But Los Angeles is a car city and Alfred didn't drive, so our second move after our first move was to get him behind the wheel. Fearlessly, he took the necessary lesson. Scared to death, I (a driver since the age of sixteen) sat in the other seat, and naturally the first night out a cop stopped us. Alfred prepared himself. The cop approached him with the usual questions. Alfred had all the answers and by now the necessary papers but, puzzled, couldn't resist asking what he had done wrong. Simultaneously the officer asked if he was *the* Sheinwold — "You know," he said, "the one in the paper."

"Are you a bridge player?" Alfred asked casually.

"I sure am. Matter of fact I'm off to the bridge club when I'm finished with you. And wait till the boys hear about this!"

Again Alfred tried. "Just what did I do wrong? I'm a new driver."

"Mr. Sheinwold, would you open a hand with four points?"

"No," replied Alfred.

"Well, we don't drive around at night without lights!" He walked away, chuckling to himself.

So maybe I can't write Sheinwold letters, but there are other advantages. The next thing we did after moving and securing Alfred on the freeways was to adopt two children, Ruff and Finesse, two tiny, adorable poodles who scampered about, especially when we played cards. Oh, yes, we did play cards. The poodles made the column several times for their antics during the games.

Alfred could tell from the lead that the Club suit would not break, and from the bidding West surely held all of the missing high cards. He had nine top tricks so set about making the tenth. He won the lead in his hand to preserve dummy's entries, pulled three rounds of trumps, and led the singleton 3 of Diamonds from his hand. East played the 4 as the black poodle fell into the peanuts.

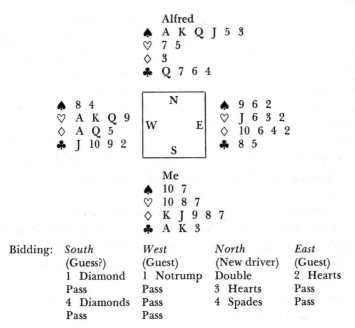

Alfred
♠ A K Q J 5 3
♡ 7 5
◇ 3
♣ Q 7 6 4

♠ 8 4
♡ A K Q 9
◇ A Q 5
♣ J 10 9 2

N
W   E
S

♠ 9 6 2
♡ J 6 3 2
◇ 10 6 4 2
♣ 8 5

Me
♠ 10 7
♡ 10 8 7
◇ K J 9 8 7
♣ A K 3

Bidding:	*South*	*West*	*North*	*East*
	(Guess?)	(Guest)	(New driver)	(Guest)
	1 Diamond	1 Notrump	Double	2 Hearts
	Pass	Pass	3 Hearts	Pass
	4 Diamonds	Pass	4 Spades	Pass
	Pass	Pass		

Opening Lead: Club 8

"Finesse!" I yelled at the dog. Alfred put in the Diamond 9!
West promptly took the 9 with his Queen, but not without
giving me a look. He then cashed his two top Heart tricks and
played a third Heart, which Alfred trumped. He then crossed to
the dummy via his carefully preserved entry, the Ace of Clubs,
and led the King of Diamonds. Both dogs pounced into the pop-
corn and I screamed, "Ruff! Finesse!"

If West covered the King, Alfred could ruff it, making his
Jack good; if West ducked, Alfred could finesse him for the Ace.
This is a complex ruffing-finesse situation that my husband could
play in his sleep, but try to explain that to the two new
friends. What was explained to me later that night was that the
dogs should be kept outside or their names changed. I opted
for outside.

We had barely settled in or had a swim when it was time to take off for the Spring Nationals. I was defending some championship or other and it's good form to show up with the same partner and put your title on the line. So as I prepared the dogs for our departure, Alfred prepared himself. Not for the unexpected turn of events at the tournament but the usual events surrounding a busy columnist. His column, "Sheinwold on Bridge," is read in about four hundred newspapers all over the world. Although it does not appear daily in all papers, in some it does, which means it has to be written. Seven days a week, seven different hands, seven different texts, which always include Alfred's erudite humor. One night at dinner we were comparing notes with Art Buchwald, who questioned how Alfred could knock out a column seven days a week when sometimes he, Art, had difficulty doing one three times weekly. We all finally agreed on the answer. When the subject matter is clearly defined you just go about it, but in Art's case, being free to write just about anything he wants can be too free. It's a sort of freedom that binds.

So I was learning just how difficult it was for Alfred to leave his typewriter and files for a ten-day stint away from home. The column is usually delivered six weeks ahead of publication, the hands being sent in a week or so before the text. Occasionally a hand would be safely in the hands of the syndicate, ready for print, when closer examination of the text would reveal certain discrepancies. And with no way to change the hand! This was always a good time for the poodles and me to hit the beach. The crime had been committed and now Alfred had to construct the proper punishment.

Another kind of punishment was sometimes inflicted on us. The column would appear and contain a typographical error. Alfred would look at me and moan. This type of printer's error would mean hundreds of letters to the columnist about *his* mistake. Bridge players love to catch others in mistakes, so we would grit our teeth for the onslaught of mail. I'd try to console him with words like: "Well, look how many people read the column!" Eventually we had explanatory cards printed, stocked up on postage, and answered the mail that way.

Besides being a syndicated columnist, Alfred is the bridge reporter for the *Los Angeles Times*. So at tournaments, when the bridge players are finally tucked in for the night, Alfred's job commences: sending home up-to-the-minute reports. This is done by phone, to be received by an electronic gismo at the other end.

With all of this going on, how could I chide him for leaving on our electric blanket? I had won it as first prize at the Northern Virginia Women's Pair Championship and didn't feel like going back there to win another. Oh, well, I consoled myself, sunny Southern California — who needs an electric blanket. All of these thoughts were flitting across my mind as we walked into the hotel lobby, our home away from home for the next ten days, a Spring Nationals.

Alfred is a very distinguished-looking man, with gray in the right spots, black-framed glasses, and the proper clipped British accent to go with his looks. Since he was born in London, the accent is as natural as the graying hair. He was easily recognized by his fans as soon as he stepped into the lobby, so while he was answering questions and autographing books, I was spelling our name for the room clerk. His next duty was to set himself up in the Press Room and make friends with the electronic gismo while I set myself up with a partner. A telegram had brought the news that my defending partner was ill and could not defend. What to do? It takes years to develop a good partnership, right? One with confidence, understanding of nuances, systemic preferences worked out over endless hands, speaking the same language and understanding it. I had two choices. One, to withdraw, or two, find the impossible. I did the latter.

Who would know how to play Alfred's way? (I had played

enough with him to understand all of the above.) Who could have been trained and taught by him, and would in turn desire what I had to offer? An ex-wife, that's who. The former Mrs. Sheinwold, now Mrs. Kaplan, was a walking system all by herself.

"You're doing what, with whom?" her ex, my present, gulped.

"You've got it." I laid it on him from behind the bathroom door and quickly turned on the water.

But Alfred is a bridge player, a sympathetic soul, and though he wondered what the hell Betty and I would talk about between hands, he did give us his blessing. When Alfred and Edgar Kaplan conceived their system, K-S, as it is commonly referred to, they were still playing as partners, but now the distaff side was taking over. The press went wild, the kibitzers formed fan clubs, the male bridgers either commiserated with Alfred and Edgar or volunteered to shoot us, and our opponents went crazy.

For you see, in a tournament each player is required to fill out a convention card. The top line requests your name, the line directly under it, your system. Our card read:

> *Name:* Kaplan-Sheinwold
> *Approach:* Modified Roth-Stone System

Each round our opponents would reach the table, look at us, and say, "Well, we know what system you're playing!" Betty and I would shove the card under their noses, but Kaplan-Sheinwold was all they ever saw. Because the K-S system lowers the usual 16–18 high-card points for 1 Notrump openings to 12–14 high-card points, whenever a K-S player opens 1 Notrump the opponents always feel they are being done in. To compensate for this they hop into the bidding, usually regardless of their point count.

Betty and I went along playing, the opponents went on hopping into the bidding, and after the disaster they would accuse

us of having more than 14 points. Again, we would gently shove
the card at them (Roth-Stone opens with 16–18). One woman
in absolute disgust asked, "Just which one of you is Mrs. Sheinwold and which one is Mrs. Kaplan?"

With complete aplomb Betty pointed to me: "That is Mrs.
Sheinwold, but I am Mrs. Kaplan-Sheinwold."

We did not disgrace ourselves or our husbands. In all sessions
we managed to stay in the top ten. Our final standing was
either three or six; I can't remember which, because one of those
numbers has been pointed out to me by a numerologist as *my*
number. Of course, the numerologist would be thrilled to know
I can't remember. At the races or other games of chance I've
solved it by playing both numbers, but the correct information
about the tournament eludes me. In a National Tournament it
is consoling to be in the top ten; competition is so fierce you can
consider yourself a winner by just being there.

Alfred asked how I liked playing with his ex, so it seemed like
a good time to tell him we were playing again, the following day,
in a team game.

"After all," I was quick to point out, "anyone you would be
married to for twenty-five years has to be nice."

When the dust from the team game had blown away, Betty
Kaplan and Patricia Sheinwold plus teammates had won. I gave
some thought to quitting tournament bridge forever. There
didn't seem to be any way to ever top this. Alfred was quite
amused to have his two wives as National Champions, and that
night as he phoned in the story to the electronic gismo it seemed
to be talking back in disbelief. Edgar Kaplan took it all in
stride, too, and was very helpful in sorting out any bidding
problems that could have arisen between us. So our first National as Mr. and Mrs. was over and we returned home to Ruff
and Finesse and ruff and finesse.

I guess when you move to a new city you finally belong when

you find a hairdresser you love. It's a different love from the school you settle on for the kids, or a laundry man or cleaner. If your clothes are destroyed by your choosing the wrong establishment, they can always be replaced. But your hair is another thing. So it was with great glee that I discovered the House of Alan Thomas. Alan and Thomas were co-owners along with Dee, Thomas's wife, who oversaw the whole operation. Their salon is nestled between a garden and two restaurants, one Mexican and one French. These make it difficult to stay on a diet, as lunch is provided if you just think about it. It is not unusual to sit under the dryer next to Peggy Cass, Patty Duke, or other film notables. The salon also features kind of a house clairvoyant, who will predict your future while you're waiting to be combed out. Naturally, the three owners are bridge players. One day, seated in front of their huge fireplace, I was working on this book when Alan sauntered by.

"Alan, I need some help. What's a finesse?"

He thought for a few seconds and said, "A finesse is when you are in One Notrump and you need another trick, you look around for it."

"Is that all?"

"I think so," he said.

"Who taught you that?"

"Dee," he said, and scurried away.

I found Dee in the back room having her future predicted and put the question to her, again asking for help with the book.

"Well," she said, "it's when you have an Ace-Queen-Jack and you want to get rid of the King."

"Right," I said. "What do you do?"

"You lay down the Queen and after someone takes it the other cards are good."

She was on the right track but on the left side of it. Just for fun, see if you can define a finesse in twenty-five words or less.

It's really not enough just to be able to do it — you should be able to define or explain it.

"Who taught you?" I continued.

"Thomas did," she said proudly.

I then sought out the culprit, Thomas, who gave me a very clear definition of a finesse. Alan overheard him, along with Dee, so they both came running to defend their positions. I hadn't meant to cause a disturbance in the quiet House of Alan Thomas, but there was quite an uproar. Their answers reminded me of a game we played as children. The first person whispers something to another, who repeats it to another, and this continues around the room until the last person says it aloud. There is never any resemblance to the original statement. And so with the garbled finesse. Have you finished your definition? It's not easy.

Sheinwold, *Five Weeks to Winning Bridge:* "The finesse, one of the basic maneuvers of bridge, is an attempt to win a trick with a card that is not the highest card of its suit *after one opponent has already played to the trick.*"

Webster, *New International Dictionary, Second Edition, Unabridged:* "The ability to handle delicate and difficult situations skillfully and diplomatically."

They're both right.

Many years of playing bridge and many years of playing bridge with other men had indeed prepared me for many years of playing with my husband, the expert. I think it is safe to say our disputes were confined to either misunderstandings of our system or a misconstruing of high-level bids. I think it is also safe to say that Alfred and I never had a fight over a bridge game. We had mutual respect for each other's ability and knew we were always on the same team. When you learn to trust and listen to your partner, you can sit back and learn to enjoy one of the best card games ever invented. Then reap the rewards of playing bridge with your favorite partner, be it spouse, lover, or friend. And when you have learned what an important role ego plays in the game and put it in its proper place, you will be a well-adjusted partner — not only at the table but everywhere.

Our bridge-playing days together were spent with the many new friends we met in California and abroad. I would now like to tell you about some of them, the bridge hands, and maybe a few anecdotes along the way.

16—

Trio Con Brio

First Movement

THE CELLO when held by Gregor Piatigorsky looks like a diminutive instrument. For, indeed, it is being held by a giant. Greek mythology tells us the giants warred with the gods; not so in the case of this giant, who explains and performs the godliness of Brahms, Bach, and Beethoven. I didn't know what to expect as Alfred and I made our way to our first encounter with him at the card table.

"Do you think it's okay if I tell him I have loved him all of my life?" I asked my spouse.

"Well, I don't know if that's the best opening line. Try 'How do you do,' " he replied.

So I said, "How do you do. I've been in love with you all my life." And from Mr. Piatigorsky I got my first Russian bear hug.

Living in Southern California puts one in constant elbow-rubbing position with stars, superstars, and giants. They are in the markets, on the beaches, in the department stores, seated next to you at the theater and at concerts. It takes a while to get used to it. One of our first informal dinners found me explaining to Budd Schulberg the intricacies of opening a Maryland hard-shell crab. I would have preferred asking him about his books, but you learn to check your enthusiastic leanings. We shared a gardener with Paul and Joanne Newman and Doris Day. And our over-the-fence neighbor for ten years was Hedy Lamarr, while Ben Gazzara was "running for his life" at the corner. But in the case of Gregor Piatigorsky I just couldn't help myself.

So as the cards were dealt I fought savagely to keep my mind and eyes on the happy spots. I sneaked a glance at his hands. They are so beautifully large he could palm all thirteen if he wanted to.

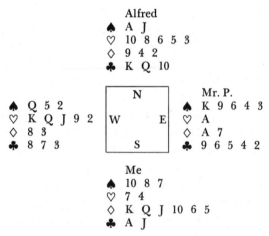

Alfred
♠ A J
♡ 10 8 6 5 3
◇ 9 4 2
♣ K Q 10

♠ Q 5 2
♡ K Q J 9 2
◇ 8 3
♣ 8 7 3

Mr. P.
♠ K 9 6 4 3
♡ A
◇ A 7
♣ 9 6 5 4 2

Me
♠ 10 8 7
♡ 7 4
◇ K Q J 10 6 5
♣ A J

Declarer: South
Opening Lead: Heart King

Alfred and I found ourselves in the somewhat shaky contract of 3 Notrump. The hand could produce nine tricks once the Ace of Diamonds was knocked out: three Clubs, five Diamonds, one Spade. Mr. Piatigorsky's partner led the King of Hearts, dummy played low, while Mr. P. was forced to play the Ace. I heaved a sigh of relief as the play of the Ace, to use a bridge player's expression, put pants on the 10.

"Do you know where the expression 'to lose your head in love' originated?" Mr. Piatigorsky asked me.

"I don't think so."

"Well," he continued, "the female praying mantis is known to decapitate her suitors, and perhaps it was those beheaded males who are responsible for the old saying. And being a male I am going in search of a female." He then laid down the King of Spades.

It didn't make a bit of difference whether I won the Spade then or later. He had created an entry to his partner's hand via the Queen of Spades. Before I could knock out the Diamond Ace and take my tricks, they could now cash the Queen-Jack of Hearts, the Spade Queen, and the Diamond Ace for down one. His analysis of the hand was as accurate as his reading of any musical score, and his timing was just as perfect.

"How does it feel to be da capo by someone you've loved all your life?" asked Alfred.

My emotions were mixed. It is never totally deflating to be defeated by a master play, only deflating to be in a shaky contract when you are supposedly a good player.

"Mr. Piatigorsky, you just executed a Deschapelles Coup against me. I commend you."

"One learns a lot about communication and timing making music," he said with a smile, "and you may call me Grisha."

I fell in love all over again — even without my head.

The Deschapelles Coup was so named for Guillaume le Breton Deschapelles (1780–1847), reputedly the greatest whist player of his time. The play calls for the sacrificial endeavor of an unsupported high honor card by you in order to establish an honor in your partner's hand.

Second Movement

When Alfred is not tra-la-la-ing at the typewriter he is tra-la-la-ing at lieder. He has a nice tenor range and treats Schubert gently as only a gentleman should. When I'm not pondering a bridge hand I'm pounding the piano. And not so gently. When Leonard Pennario is not concertizing, he is practicing. When he is not practicing, he is studying. And when he's not doing any of the above, he is playing bridge. We became a menagerie à trois always seeking le quarte; Leonard produced les quartes, usually from the world of music. What excitement to find fourths at his home the likes of John Browning, Thomas Schippers, and Alfred Wallenstein.

Between tours Leonard would regale us with stories about his musical wanderings and bridge meanderings, all brought together by means of jet transportation.

"It's a great way to travel," he said. "It makes it now possible to play in Oklahoma City one day and Milano the next. Only thing is, jets do have a lot of delays."

I was musing over this one night at the table with Leonard as my partner. Leonard opened the bidding with 1 Spade.

This is an extremely delicate hand. You might want to cover the East-West cards and play it for yourself before continuing. I was glad it was in hands of an equally delicate nature. Leonard won the lead perforce in the dummy with the Ace, because a Diamond switch by East would have brought instant defeat. But now comes the delicate part. He must arrange to get back and forth from dummy to his hand to repeat the Heart finesse for the King. And he cannot pull trumps first or he will be locked in the dummy with only one entry to his hand. Very delicate, indeed. Leonard played the Spade 8 and overtook it with his Jack, then took the first Heart finesse. Next he played the Spade 9 from dummy and overtook it with his Spade King

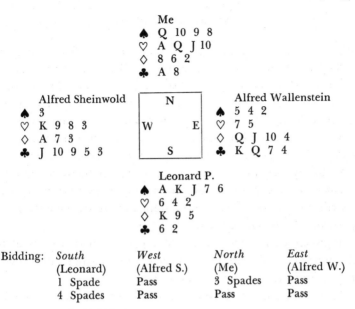

Me
- ♠ Q 10 9 8
- ♡ A Q J 10
- ◇ 8 6 2
- ♣ A 8

Alfred Sheinwold
- ♠ 3
- ♡ K 9 8 3
- ◇ A 7 3
- ♣ J 10 9 5 3

Alfred Wallenstein
- ♠ 5 4 2
- ♡ 7 5
- ◇ Q J 10 4
- ♣ K Q 7 4

Leonard P.
- ♠ A K J 7 6
- ♡ 6 4 2
- ◇ K 9 5
- ♣ 6 2

Bidding:	*South*	*West*	*North*	*East*
	(Leonard)	(Alfred S.)	(Me)	(Alfred W.)
	1 Spade	Pass	3 Spades	Pass
	4 Spades	Pass	Pass	Pass

Opening Lead: Club Jack

in order to repeat the Heart finesse. Once more, he played the Spade 10 and overtook it with his Ace. After one more Heart finesse, he cashed the Ace of Hearts and tossed his losing Club for a total of ten tricks.

"Bravo!" we all exclaimed.

"It looks as if your jet delays helped with the trump delays, to say nothing about the way you arranged your transportation," I observed.

And Leonard replied, "In the manner of making music one learns a lot about transportation and delays." I thought about the transportation of his fingers on the keyboard.

"The performer learns *ritardando* just as the bridge player does," Alfred added.

Leonard went to the piano, Alfred began to sing, and I began to wonder why so many musicians play bridge and why so many bridge players are musicians.

Third Movement

If anyone had ever told me I would be playing Ping-Pong in the house of Jascha Heifetz in Jascha Heifetz's shirt with him as my partner I wouldn't have believed it in this world or in any other karmic adventure.

Leonard had introduced us to him as people first, card players second, and music aficionados third. So it seemed reasonable to assume we were invited to his home on the first two counts. I was busy scurrying around the bedroom rejecting every outfit I had owned since college, even the new one I had bought for the occasion. In the final few seconds I settled for a heavy, long-sleeved sweater and matching slacks. As we approached the front gate we were confronted by a Beware of Dog sign. Alfred sensibly backed off but I plowed right in. Anyone who could cope with Ruff and Finesse could cope with any four-legged beast. This one turned out to be His Master's Voice, RCA's famous trademark — in cardboard! I made a mental note about Mr. Heifetz's humor.

He greeted us warmly as he introduced us to his other guest. See, I was right; four for bridge. Wrong. He asked if we played paddle tennis, for he had a court in the back. Oh dear God, I thought, I play tennis, golf, basketball, baseball, polo, swim, ride, bowl — how in the hell did I miss paddle tennis! I was feeling like an idiot when he asked about Ping-Pong. Reinstated. We started to play but the heat generated from the sweater was too much, and that's how I ended up in his shirt. Alfred, being British, thought I should have stuck it out in my sweater, but you know how we colonists are.

Mr. Heifetz is a first-class Ping-Ponger, with great concentration and excellent timing. After this premeal warmup we dined and wined, preparing, I thought, for the postmeal bridge game.

"Do you play spite and malice?" he asked as we approached the card table.

Ye Gods, I thought, I play gin, poker, bridge, canasta, old maid, casino, solo, hearts — even fifty-two pickup — how could I have missed spite and malice!

"I'll teach you another time," he said. "Let's play gin."

We cut for partners and decided on Hollywood* — a good choice considering we were in Beverly Hills — combined with Oklahoma† — as long as we were in California! It was obvious we were in a very professional game by the discard pile. Non-players either keep the pile strewn all over the table or permit digging back into it for a look. This is unthinkable in a good game, where only the top card is visible in an otherwise neatly maintained pile. One of the important elements of good gin is to remember every card you and your opponents discard. Equally important, you must remember the discards your opponent refuses as well as the ones he takes.

One of my first discards to Mr. Heifetz, which he grabbed, was the Jack of Diamonds, at that point in the game a relatively safe discard. It was only after the hand that I realized why he had picked it up. He had held the Queen, 9, 8 of Diamonds. His maneuver was tricky and good. After he picked up the Jack, I was then forced to hold on to future Jacks. But he added 50 per cent to his chances because he could now use the King, 10, 7 of Diamonds, where before he picked up the Jack he could have only used the 10 or 7. He was indeed a player, not someone out for an outing.

Sometimes in gin you are confronted with the miserable decision of having to give your opponent a card he needs. I was standing behind Mr. H. when Alfred was his opponent. Alfred's hand:

* Three games played simultaneously.
† Spades double.

Clubs: Q J 10
Hearts: 6 5
Spades: 6
Diamonds: 5 4
plus an odd Ace and Deuce

Mr. Heifetz had the miserable choice of discarding either the Club 9 or the Diamond 3. Which one would you discard and why? He correctly discarded the Club 9. This could only extend Alfred's set, not make a new one for him. It left the 5 and 4 of Diamonds still at sea. Alfred and I exchanged one of those all-knowing looks that accompany a close relationship. It was fun playing the game well against someone who plays his thing well.

By the time the evening was over we both thought we had pegged Mr. Heifetz's game, so when we were invited to play again we were prepared. Well, not exactly. Mr. Heifetz varies his style. As one has to learn style variation when playing Mozart one day and Bruch the next, so he did in gin. (Again, this is the mark of a good player.) Future games included the other two thirds of the trio, Mr. Piatigorsky and Mr. Pennario, plus very dear friends, the Chapro family. We were playing six-handed and two of the pairs had finished, so I glanced at Mr. Heifetz's hand as he prepared to discard (we were teammates). After ten picks his hand:

Three Kings
Two 7 (Heart and Diamond)
Matching Q J 10
And the odd 9 and 3 both needed by his opponent

He drew the Heart 8 (this went nicely with his 7). But he varied his play and discarded the 8! This is not only good form but the correct line of play, as a team member. The necessary ingredient of a good chamber music teammate, also?

Back home I asked Alfred if he had noticed how extraordinary

Mr. Heifetz's memory was. He had, and added the words concentration, tenacity, and timing. Before dousing the light Alfred asked me if I had forgotten what is required in the business of making music à la Heifetz.

Eventually I asked Mr. Heifetz about bridge. He had played many years ago, but one evening he was made to feel so uncomfortable by two other players who were arguing with each other that he didn't want to witness it again. I reminded him of the time Nathan Milstein walked out on the Pittsburgh Symphony and its conductor, William Steinberg.

"I didn't give up on them and never intend to."

"Well," he said, "this altercation happened many years ago. Maybe someday I will play bridge again."

Unfortunately this is the cry of many ex-bridgers whose experiences at the table have had lasting effects. But in the case of Mr. Heifetz I can't help feeling that the game of bridge lost a friend and that a friend lost many hours of pleasurable card-playing.

Coda

Paderewski and Rachmaninoff were bridge players. Abram Chasins, pianist, composer, author, musicologist, is a bridge player, as is his wife, concert pianist Constance Keene. Eugene Istomin, pianist with the famous Istomin-Stern-Rose Trio, and John Lewis, pianist and founder of the Modern Jazz Quartet, are both bridgers. Edgar and Betty Kaplan are musicians, and so are countless other bridge players. Accident or coincidence?

Both require discipline brought about through love and respect for what one does. And in being disciplined, the trained mind becomes a treasure chest of experience and of memory. And with each replay a flashlight goes on, shedding even more light. To be at the right place for the right reasons calls for exact timing, and through your sense of transportation you know where to be and how to get there. Neither can work without communication: the need and desire to impart what you know and feel. The virtuoso performer either in a recital or in handling the dummy must summon all his technique to be in command. The chamber music participant requires both individual ability and a sure sense of ensemble, of partnership, of give and take — as in bridge.

Put it all together, shuffle the deck, and out comes Sigmund Romberg playing bridge with Otto Harbach. Mr. Romberg is playing the hand; Mr. Harbach is the dummy. The former had forgotten to pull the last trump, so the latter began to hum "One Alone" from *The Desert Song,* the 1926 musical in which they collaborated. Mr. Romberg plays on, oblivious of the humming hint, and goes down.

MR. HARBACH: Sigmund, didn't you hear what I was humming?

MR. ROMBERG: Yes, Otto, I did.

MR. HARBACH: Well, why didn't you pull the last trump?

MR. ROMBERG: Otto, I only wrote the music; you wrote the words.

17 —

The Mayor of Woodland Hills

WHEN I WAS a little girl back in Baltimore, almost every Saturday morning I would go to the Hippodrome Theatre. There amid spotlights, microphones, and assorted musicians Baltimore's young hopefuls would perform for Uncle Jack, whose "Kiddie Show" was broadcast weekly from the mammoth stage. I was a dancer — hardly the right medium for radio — but toeshoes in hand I would pursue my course. Each week I would stare with green-eyed envy at Ginger Dulo, star. It was a combination of instant hate and protracted admiration. So wasn't it quite natural thirty years later to find her sitting across from me eating chow mein in Los Angeles? And wouldn't it follow that she is a bridge player?

I managed to forgive her, but only because she did go on to greater heights and fame on stage and TV as Jane, not Ginger. Any night you can dial to her as Jack Benny's housekeeper, the nurse on *McHale's Navy*, the gal under the cake that Martha Raye baked on her head, or the marvelous wino on Ben Casey. As individual as she was on the screen, her bidding was just as unique. Another unusual part of her game was the manner in which she always ended up as the dummy; she hardly ever played a hand. A little research led Alfred and me down one of the most interesting bridge roads in our careers.

Jane hadn't played bridge for twenty years when suddenly she found herself on tour in *Merton of the Movies*. And the star — Buster Keaton. By the time Jane entered Buster Keaton's life he was a confirmed player, intent on making everyone around him a fiend. Even his wife, Eleanor, became a bridge player after she met him. And his sister, Louise, a bridge nut.

"We played auction, no point count, and Buster played all the hands," Jane told me.

"Didn't it ever occur to you that maybe you should play some of the hands?" we asked her.

"Not for a long time. You see, Buster liked to play everything in Notrump. So he always bid Notrump first and we let him play it there."

That statement had a familiar ring to it.

"I had played Culbertson, knew about other systems, but we were very happy playing the Buster system," she continued. "He was a fierce competitor and loved the game almost as much as he loved his work."

Many years later the Keatons and Ginger-Jane settled in California and resumed their bridge games. They played every Sunday, all day and night, and on holidays, breaking only for cocktail time, not for any new arrivals — nothing interfered with their bridge.

Buster, being a fan of the column, was delighted to learn that Jane knew us, and a game was promptly arranged. We arrived at his home completely aware that Buster Keaton was a highly inventive man, full of daring, and one of the great creators of his time. For it was common knowledge that he not only created his stunts but performed them — there were no stand-ins. He was responsible for the use of the comedy camera at standard speed rather than the crazily stepped-up motion of the old Keystone Kops comedies.

So why not this play against us? Inventive, daring, and like his work, very well thought out.

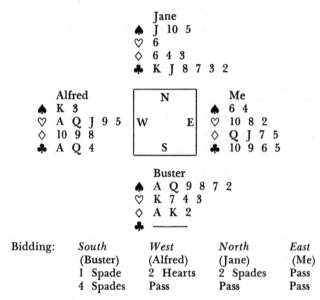

Jane
♠ J 10 5
♡ 6
◇ 6 4 3
♣ K J 8 7 3 2

Alfred
♠ K 3
♡ A Q J 9 5
◇ 10 9 8
♣ A Q 4

Me
♠ 6 4
♡ 10 8 2
◇ Q J 7 5
♣ 10 9 6 5

Buster
♠ A Q 9 8 7 2
♡ K 7 4 3
◇ A K 2
♣ ——

Bidding:	South	West	North	East
	(Buster)	*(Alfred)*	*(Jane)*	*(Me)*
	1 Spade	2 Hearts	2 Spades	Pass
	4 Spades	Pass	Pass	Pass

Opening Lead: Diamond 10

As Alfred led the Diamond 10 I smiled at Jane-dummy, because Buster was in 4 Spades, not Notrump. Buster looked at the dummy, thought for a few minutes, and called for the 3; I played the 7, and he played simultaneously the Diamond King and the Heart King! A touch of comedy but, oh, so shrewd. He won the trick with the Diamond King and left the Heart King on the table. It was the only card he could play to make his contract. Alfred's overcall of Hearts had marked him with the

Ace and it was important to put him on lead. There was nothing Alfred could do. If he returned a trump, dummy would be able to ruff only twice but the trump King would be sacrificed. If Alfred returned anything else, Buster could ruff his three losing Hearts and give up a Diamond and trump at the end.

"Beautiful play," Alfred said. "If you had led a low Heart, Pat would have won it and switched to a trump, then you'd have gone down. Your play guaranteed the contract against any defense."

"I got a fortunate opening lead," Buster said quietly. He was careful not to tread too heavily on Alfred's toes.

But later that night Alfred remarked to me how surprised he was that Buster picked up on the unfortunate lead so quickly. The killing lead is a trump, but only after you see the dummy can you spot it. Buster could win the trump lead and play a Heart, but continuation of the trump suit prevents him from ruffing three Hearts. True, the defense loses a trump trick, but it picks up the additional Heart tricks.

Back in the days when people crossed the country by train, time was passed by playing cards. Buster was on such a trip when he was conned into a game by some of the top Hollywood producers. His knowledge of the game was nil and so was his wallet when he reached New York. The stakes were high and Buster's mistakes filled the kitty. His determination took over, so in New York he holed up and learned the game. Armed with his wits, talent, and new-found ability, he boarded the train for the return trip. He planned to play only one session, recoup his money, and quit. The biggies rolled up their sleeves for the kill, but this time it was Buster who did the killing. The only thing that went wrong with his plan was, he got hooked on bridge forever.

When things were tough, Buster could make a living playing bridge at Hillcrest Country Club, the club of the Hollywood tycoons. It didn't take the movie colony long to discover he was one of its best players, but he limited his stakes to only a penny game. If the game was played for higher stakes the kibitzers could pick up the difference. P. Hal Sims, then reigning monarch of bridge, had a standing side bet on Keaton. He stood 6 feet 4 inches tall, tipping the scale at over 300 pounds, and no one was about to deny him his wish to keep a standing bet on Buster — only a monarch in his own right — Louis B. Mayer, king of the film industry. Mayer paid Keaton a tribute by cutting the game to a penny, Buster's stake.

"He didn't mind losing to me. There was nothing cheap about Mayer," Buster told us. "He just saw no reason to support the people who were betting on me."

As the stunt man lives dangerously, so does the bridge player. But to stay alive both rely on timing and judgment. Buster was sitting South in his favorite contract of 3 Notrump (the bidding having gone 1 Notrump–3 Notrump). I was on lead with the following hand. What would you lead?

> Spades: J 8 6 2
> Hearts: Q 9
> Diamonds: 10 7
> Clubs: A Q J 10 9

This seemed to me the time to live dangerously, deceptively, and, I hoped, successfully. You never know when you make a lead such as the Queen of Clubs if it will win or backfire. It could possibly give declarer his ninth trick or cause him consternation.

Buster played low; Alfred, not wishing me to make an unfortunate switch, played his 7. The play of the 7 was just what the doctor ordered to carry on with the deception, so I whipped out the Jack. Now it was Buster's turn to make his decision. If I had led from five Clubs then Alfred's Ace was third, and Buster

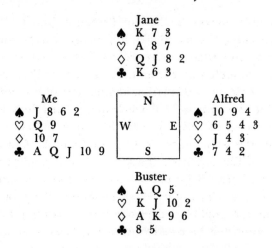

Jane
♠ K 7 3
♡ A 8 7
♢ Q J 8 2
♣ K 6 3

Me
♠ J 8 6 2
♡ Q 9
♢ 10 7
♣ A Q J 10 9

Alfred
♠ 10 9 4
♡ 6 5 4 3
♢ J 4 3
♣ 7 4 2

Buster
♠ A Q 5
♡ K J 10 2
♢ A K 9 6
♣ 8 5

could block the suit by ducking again, as Alfred would be unable
to put me back in. But if I had led from the Ace — well, what
to do? He ducked. We took five tricks for down one. Buster
didn't move a muscle in his face; he didn't even write down the
score. He leaned over to the floor, took a firm grasp on an imaginary pie, came up slowly, and threw it in my face. I wiped the
gook from my eyes with both hands, staring at him as intensely
as I could and matching him look for look, and handed him
the pencil. As Jane said, "He never misses. Best aim in the
business."

Buster hated to lose at bridge, but he respected professional-
ism. Eleanor, his wife, told us about the hours he would spend
thinking out his material.

"He left nothing to chance and never pulled surprises; furthermore," Eleanor added, "he also liked to build sets and
props. He enjoyed working his tail off."

The first time Buster stood up and said he was going down
to the saloon for a drink, Alfred and I thought he was leaving
the game for a snort somewhere in Woodland Hills, the Hills be-

ing one of many towns in the San Fernando Valley. There's Encino, Van Nuys, Sherman Oaks, and many others — all make up the valley. But what he did was walk about six feet to his bar and pour himself a beer from the spigoted vat that rested at the far end. This was a Busterism, another one of his endearing qualities. Buster was never a name-dropper, but a look around the room reflected the many greats with whom he had worked. Hanging on the walls were the faces of Chaplin, Laurel and Hardy, Harold Lloyd, Fatty Arbuckle, each autographed with a reference or tribute to Buster. Sometimes Buster would walk around with us relating a story about the face in the photograph or explaining the trophies and plaques. He was losing his hearing at this point, but he could read in our faces what we were thinking.

He was an unusually strong man, having been a first-rate tumbler in earlier days, and he adored sports. He was also an unusually gentle man, yet very much the head of his family. He played the ukulele and loved to sing old songs. Often he could be found just wandering around the baby department in one of the local Woodland Hills stores. Another favorite pasttime was romping with dogs. His own was a Saint Bernard, Junior, who I swear had the same look on his face as Buster. Junior thought nothing of climbing onto your lap once he knew you, especially in the middle of a hand. It was like having another opponent. Or maybe Buster trained him to go into his act when the opponents were about to make a game against him. Buster was one of the true people. We asked one of his children what they admired most about him and the answer was: "He never gives a dishonest answer."

Although he hated losing at bridge, he was delighted when his pupils, Eleanor and Jane, beat him. He preferred small groups of people, no talk about the old days, and although he had no formal schooling he had a Master's and Ph.D. in life education.

Shortly before his death he, Eleanor, and Jane came to our house to dine and play our last game together. He adored Chinese food and that was the tone of the evening. Even the bridge game had an Oriental flavor.

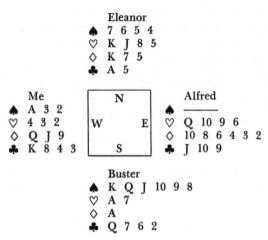

Eleanor
♠ 7 6 5 4
♡ K J 8 5
◊ K 7 5
♣ A 5

Me
♠ A 3 2
♡ 4 3 2
◊ Q J 9
♣ K 8 4 3

Alfred
♠ —
♡ Q 10 9 6
◊ 10 8 6 4 3 2
♣ J 10 9

Buster
♠ K Q J 10 9 8
♡ A 7
◊ A
♣ Q 7 6 2

Contract: 6 Spades
Opening Lead: Diamond Queen

Buster, sitting South, won the opening lead in his hand. He studied the dummy and then laid down the Queen of Clubs! There was no way I was going to cover it with my King to set up the Jack-10, which I assumed he held. Why take such a finesse except to then discard what I thought was a losing Diamond. So I ducked, his Queen held, he gave me the Spade Ace, and that was the end of the hand — he threw one losing Club on the King of Diamonds and trumped the other.

"That dinner was really food for thought," quipped Alfred.

"Nice play" was all I could manage, wiping the Egg Foo Young off my face. In bridge Buster's inspired play is known as a Chinese finesse: the attempt to win a trick with unsupported honors.

While still alive, Buster was given the title Mayor of Woodland Hills. When he died, a deck of cards was placed in the coffin.

I think Jane's words best describe him: "He was a man of genius, good taste, never vulgar, with a great sense of satire which dealt with people; he showed the plight of man from royalty to tramp."

And he was sweet and kind. The doorbell rang one Sunday afternoon and Eleanor found two nine-year-olds pleading, "Please Mrs. Keaton, can Buster come out to play?"

The seventy-year-old Buster grinned from ear to ear as he bounced out the door to play baseball with his friends. We understood. It was bridge he loved, but kids and baseball he adored.

18 —

Save the Face

"TRAVEL WITH Goren," "Travel with Sheinwold" — travel, travel, travel. Bridge went into the travel business. Its special appeal is to the single person of any age. For you are guaranteed not to be alone on a short or long cruise. "Wanna make a fourth?" is understood even in Swahili.

When the West Coast President Lines approached us to go cruising, we said "Yes" with all the excitement of two people about to go out on their first date: Japan, Australia, New Zealand, Hong Kong, New Guinea, Bali — and we would be paid to do it.

If I thought Alfred's preparation for a National Tournament was tremendous, it was nothing compared to what had to be done prior to a three-month cruise. For no matter where we were, the column still had to be written. I can still picture Alfred typing in Tahiti, punctuating in Pago Pago, bidding in Bali, augmenting in Auckland, and buying manila mailing envelopes — where else? — in Manila. My contribution to his cause was contracting flu — where else? — in Hong Kong.

Our first cruise found us with fifty avid bridge nuts. Why do I say avid? Because when we sailed through the magnificent Sea of Japan, not one player was curious enough to leave the card table. I strolled through the lounge where they were playing and calmly announced that the scenery equaled 7 Notrump, doubled, redoubled, vulnerable, and making, but not one person bothered to look or even look up.

As we were nearing Tokyo I asked Alfred if the players would be getting off the ship to see the sights.

"Of course they'll be getting off." He shot me a look I didn't quite recognize. "We're playing a friendly duplicate tournament there. Each of us Americans will be partnered with a Japanese player."

"That's a pretty sneaky way to move them out of the lounge," I said, trying to shoot back the same look. My idea of an interesting few days in Tokyo did not include playing bridge. I thought a bridge cruise meant bridge while cruising, which didn't include while cruising on land. But I soon learned that the players wanted to play — anywhere, anytime, any country, any language, any partner.

On board in the morning the players had their choice of a lecture by Sheinwold or a beginner's class given by one of our two assistants. In the afternoons and evenings there were duplicate and/or rubber games. All games were supervised by one of us or we'd make a fourth when needed.

Sometimes the running of the game or even the participation in one required the diplomatic know-how of twenty years in the Foreign Service. Whether you're an expert or not, being in the middle of an argument between two hostile people can be very sticky. Alfred has come up with a few beautiful solutions: "I never give bidding advice on hands containing nine-card suits" or "If my partner leaves me in a ridiculous contract I get up from the table and let him play it." Mine is much more uncivilized. I cop out by saying: "I don't know." Whichever way you choose, stay out of it. You're bound to make at least one enemy. Occasionally you might come across two mentally balanced, ego-sound people; then, and only then, do you give an opinion. And then you'll probably end up with half an enemy.

"Alfred, do you think Mr. Willey really threw his wife overboard?"

"I didn't hear any ship signal. Maybe he just held her head under the shower."

"That's worse. She just had her hair done!"

Mrs. Willey had attended one of the morning beginner's classes. Mr. Willey was at Alfred's lecture. In the afternoon the bidding between them went 1 Notrump by her, 2 Spades by him, Pass, Pass, Pass. Mrs. Willey had learned something new, applied it to their game, but forgot to tell Mr. Willey, who was still waiting for her to bid over his 2 Spades. Well, they're both right, but who was going to tell them? Especially when one of them was missing.

"How do you arrive at an understanding?" I asked Alfred.

"Discuss it first. You know that."

The Willeys' bidding is a very common misunderstanding at the table, and it must be clarified or you'll end up with only a very shaky foot on the ground. Most people play that any 2-level bid over an opening of 1 Notrump shows a weak hand (unless you are using a convention). But there are still some diehards who play it forcing on one hand and not forcing on the other. How you figure it out is beyond me. If you have opened 1 Notrump and partner responds 2 of anything, there is one exception and one only. As opener, your hand should contain 18 high-card points and two of the top three honor cards in the suit named by partner. Then and only then can you speak again. And when you speak, you may only raise partner's suit, not bid any more Notrump. It is then up to partner. You have told your story, so don't turn into a filibustering bidder.

So Mrs. Willey went to the class and learned the above; when her husband bid 2 Spades, armed with her new information she left him there. And it was then and there he threatened to toss her overboard. She was right but so was he. They had been playing their Mamma-Poppa way for twenty years. How was he supposed to know she had changed their system as well as her hairdo midsea?

Partner opens the bidding with 1 Notrump and you hold:

```
       Spades:  10 9 x x x x x
       Hearts:  x
     Diamonds:  x x
        Clubs:  x x x
```

Surely you don't want to play this hand in Notrump, but you do want to play it in Spades. The only way you can is to bid it and know partner will leave you there.

Now if partner happens to have the exception and raises you to 3 Spades you are still safe. This hand, facing 18 high-card points and two of the top three honors in Spades, cannot be in jeopardy. Make sure you've established in front which way you are playing all 2-level responses over the 1 Notrump openings. If you don't you will be in the same mess as the Willeys. If you have a pig-headed partner who pursues with a 2 Notrump rebid, then you are justified in throwing him overboard.

"How are you going to save their faces?" I asked Alfred. "It's a touchy affair between husband and wife — or any two people, for that matter."

He said he would and he did as I turned my attention to another facet of face-saving. Japan is the original "Save the Face" nation, and with me to be partnered by a new Japanese partner in the upcoming tournament, I felt it merited some thought. On foreign shores all Americans want to show pretty faces, but confronted with the great ego game of bridge it could be a problem.

Feeling more at ease when I spotted Mrs. Willey once again

under the dryer, I went to the ship's shop for a brief browse (even English was beginning to take on Oriental overtones) in search of a primer on Japanese. There it was, *Japanese in a Nutshell.* I wondered if the title had been inspired by Goren's book *Bridge in a Nutshell.* Before you could count one-two-three I had learned just that in Japanese: *ichi* (1) - *ni* (2) - *san* (3). Alfred came into the stateroom and found me sitting cross-legged on the bed reciting over and over with some fervor, *"ichi-ni-san . . ."*

"Ichi-ni-san," he picked up with characteristic cool. "Don't tell me — you have dermatitis of the knee — right?" The bridge expert is also a word maven.

A few days later we sailed into Yokohama, then went on to Tokyo by car. All of us, including both Willeys. As we dressed for the tournament I launched into my theory about saving the face — theirs, ours, America's. For you see, even a world authority, such as Alfred, when partnered with a comparative dumdum in any country, can lose. Bridge players unencumbered by anything short of a death wish always want to win.

"Bridge players can be pretty ugly; but an Ugly American player is worse than an ugly duckling player in a Mixed Pairs Event" was my opening gambit.

"That's right." He was quick to seize my thought. "And I do feel we are representing our country."

"So do you think *you* should deliver a lecture on this before the tournament?"

I had handed him a hot potato. It was almost the same as stepping into an argument between players. So before we launched into the Sea of Japanese players Alfred launched into a few words of "How To." Whether you are in Japan or in your living room, settle all bidding conventions, opening-lead conventions, defensive conventions before you deal the cards. I smiled to myself as he even delivered my old "rocking-chair theory."

After the formalities we were introduced to our partners.

Alfred cut the retired president of the Bank of Tokyo. A most genteel gentleman. I was partnered with Mrs. Kawashima. I offered my hand, she bowed, we collided, and both of us got it right in the face.

"I'm afraid I do not play your famous system, Kaplan-Sheinwold," Mrs. Kawashima said as we righted ourselves.

"That's all right. Neither do I," I said with what I hoped was a save-her-face smile.

"I read where you play equally famous system, Roth-Stone." (Aha! We're in . . . or were we?) "I do not play that either," she continued. So. Four big names in bridge down the drain.

"I play American Standard," she said proudly.

"Stan —" I caught myself (it's Standard American). I only hoped it was the same system. Not some new one dreamed up by a plumbing company in Ohio. "That's fine with me," I assured her.

As we settled ourselves at the table we discussed the ramifications of bidding, leads, etc., just as Alfred had explained at his lecture. The handwriting was clearly defined on the walls — or, in this case, the characters on the silk screen. We were playing American Standard with Blackwood. Years ago I had made my own rule never to play any unusual systems or conventions with a new partner, especially an inexperienced one. And I've remained doggedly true to it. If the player tries to insist, the dodge is easy enough: "I haven't played that convention," or "I don't think I fully understand it."

Now, ego, hear this: This doesn't mean you haven't played these particular conventions for years and years. It simply means you're cutting down on possible partnership misunderstandings. Maybe you don't look so bright, but many a bright player has lost many a dollar and many a tournament for needing to appear bright.

Of course, you could always answer your new partner with: "*I* like that convention but I don't think *we* should play it." But this carries with it a subtle insult: "Yeah, but I don't think *you* can handle it."

Mrs. Kawashima and I played happily along. American Standard held its own and then *pow*. I opened with 1 Notrump; she bid 2 Spades. I had forgotten to mention it — the very thing the Willeys had fought over. The words of Alfred came back: "Discuss it first." What to do? I looked around for Madame Butterfly's weapon. It would have been easy to do away with myself on the spot. We had discussed everything else; how in the name of the emperor could I have forgotten this? I looked at my hand: no 18 high-card points, no two of the top three Spade honors. I did the honorable thing. I passed — paying her the compliment of being a first-class player. A face-saving bid. For even if she did not understand the pass at the moment, certainly someday she would.

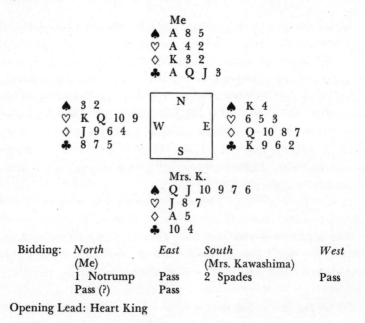

Me
♠ A 8 5
♡ A 4 2
◇ K 3 2
♣ A Q J 3

♠ 3 2
♡ K Q 10 9
◇ J 9 6 4
♣ 8 7 5

N
W   E
S

♠ K 4
♡ 6 5 3
◇ Q 10 8 7
♣ K 9 6 2

Mrs. K.
♠ Q J 10 9 7 6
♡ J 8 7
◇ A 5
♣ 10 4

Bidding:	*North* (Me)	*East*	*South* (Mrs. Kawashima)	*West*
	1 Notrump	Pass	2 Spades	Pass
	Pass (?)	Pass		

Opening Lead: Heart King

West led the King of Hearts. Mrs. Kawashima looked thoughtfully at the dummy, counting her losers: two Hearts, one Club (maybe), one Spade (maybe). She ducked the Heart lead and West shifted to the Diamond 4. The Club shift would have been useless and ill-timed, for if East holds the King he will always make it. Mrs. Kawashima won the Diamond in her hand, took the Spade finesse, which lost, and when a Heart was returned she was in a hopeless mess.

"Very nice pass, Mrs. Sheinwold," she said, as she made only three.

I was discussing the hand with Alfred later that night.

"You know," he said, "Four Spades is cold."

"Yes, I know," I replied glumly. "It was my fault for failing to discuss *it*."

"Well, it didn't matter because she only made three." He tried to console me.

"Alfred, the Japanese are truly the masters at saving face — no matter whose."

"Why do you say that?"

"Because Mrs. Kawashima has the skill to make that hand. I played all day with her, and after twenty-eight hands I think I know her ability as well as her limitations. She could have made that hand. She was saving my face from passing what *she* played as a forcing bid."

"That's nice," he said, "that's really nice.'

We went over the hand. The correct line of play is to duck the first Heart, win the Diamond switch in your hand, but *take the Club finesse first*. This enables you to keep control of the hand so when the Heart is returned you can safely win it with the Ace and discard your other losing Heart on the now high Club before you take the Spade finesse.

"Let's have a drink. Besides needing it, I can practice my Japanese." By then I had learned not only *ichi-ni-san* but *dozo* (please) and *saki* (wine). The waiter came to our table, and in my best singsong voice I said, *"Dozo, ni saki."*

He sat down with us.

"Now what do we do?" asked Alfred as calmly as possible.

"Bid Four Spades — maybe?" was all I could think of.

We have asked many Japanese why the waiter sat down, but after they stop laughing they never tell us. To the end they are the original Save-the-Face nation.

Back on the ship, all fifty accounted for, it was business as usual. Mrs. Willey had dyed her hair black for the Tokyo tournament and was seated across the table from her husband, hoping he wouldn't recognize her. Alfred and I stopped at the table long enough to hear the bidding:

Opponent	Mr. Willey	Opponent	Mrs. Willey
1 Heart	Pass	3 Hearts	3 Spades
Pass	Pass	Double	Pass
Pass	Redouble?	Pass	Pass!
Pass			

Mr. Willey turned the whitest white I have ever seen as Mrs. Willey passed his redouble. I thought it was only a matter of seconds before cardiac arrest set in. Either he would stop breathing or murder the new Cho-Cho San. His redouble says: Partner, I cannot stand the double of Spades; please bid your next best suit. In this case it would have to be Clubs or Diamonds even if she had only three in the suit — the cards are not important. Mr. Willey had the right hand on which to redouble. He was void in Spades and held five Diamonds and five Clubs, so if his partner had three of either one they would hold eight in the suit. It is not always this clear when to make the takeout redouble. The bid requires good judgment. And in this case Mrs. Willey did enter the auction alone at the three level, so she should have a good Spade suit. But he did what he thought was right. So did she when she passed; she did not want to run to another suit, for her Spade suit was solid. She made 3 Spades doubled and redoubled.

With his new-found breath, Mr. Willey said, *"Don't you ever pass my redouble again."* And that says a lot.

They both turned to Alfred. They were both right. Alfred held the hot potato again and no one was willing to grab it. Both assistants became instantly busy. I answered his pleading look with: "No potatoes for me, I'm on a diet."

There was no way Alfred could give Mr. Willey a lecture on his ego, but we both agreed his was the ego trip of all time.

"Do you really think he's going to throw her overboard?" I asked my husband later that night.

"I hope not. I hope she just gets her hair done again."

"Why's that?" I queried.

"Because I'm giving her the Most Improved Player award at the final banquet."

"That's nice," I replied, "that's very nice."

19—

Fat-Free Bridge

WE ARRIVED BACK from Japan looking unusually healthy. That is to say, Alfred looked healthy and I looked unusual. I had departed weighing a normal 125 and returned weighing . . . too much. The first night home our dear friends Mildreth and Jack Sheinkopf insisted we come over for bridge and dinner, and much to my delight, Millie had gained weight, too.

A few days later Mil called with the news that she had found a diet farm — that featured bridge. Quickly we phoned for a reservation after Alfred and Jack assured us they would come for a visit. Jack approved, Alfred helped me pack, and Ruff and Finesse went to a kennel.

"How long will you be staying?" a nice thin voice inquired.

"Fifteen pounds' worth," I answered. Mil concurred. She also agreed with me when I suggested we munch a few candy bars en route, "for God only knows when we'll eat again." A lame but convincing excuse.

The inn was located in Lancaster, California, about two hours by car from Los Angeles. The drive was a happy one, filled with thoughts of new clothes for our new figures, new bridge partners, and the consolation of all of us fatties in the same shape under the same roof. There we would be sharpening our Notrumps, bidding slams — never thinking about the enemy, food. Our only enemies would be our new opponents at the card table.

We arrived about noon. The inn, really a motel type of building, was constructed around a swimming pool. It was a beautiful, clear, 80-degree day (despite what the natives say, an unusual one for Southern California), and we wondered why no one was in the water. There were dozens of bicycles lined up like soldiers but no generals to command them. For a moment we had the horrible feeling that we were the only people there, which confirmed our feelings. We were definitely the only overweight people left in the world.

"Mil, where do you think all the people are?" I asked, dragging her back toward the car.

"In their rooms, dying of starvation." She pulled me back. "Let's check the desk."

There we were greeted by the thin telephone voice with an equally thin body. She assured us we were at the right place and reassured us we would be just as thin as the other guests in no time.

"What other guests?" one of us asked.

"Oh" — she looked up from her forms — "we're full up. You have the last two rooms." That was the best assurance we had. Others had survived or were surviving. This bit of reassurance lasted until mealtime. It is still painful to describe, but here goes.

Breakfast: Orange juice and coffee, or apple juice and coffee, or tomato juice and coffee, or just coffee. We learned after the first day to grab the juice because the total caloric intake for any day was only 150 calories. One hundred and fifty — or down three, not vulnerable, undoubled.

Lunch: A cup of bouillon, a dish of Jell-O, and black coffee. It was like a POW bill of fare. I would have preferred glucose. At least it goes into your arm and you don't have to look at it.

Dinner: There was bouillon and coffee and Jell-O; or a wee cup of stewed tomatoes and coffee and Jell-O; or a dime-sized portion of cottage cheese and bouillon and coffee.

"Mildreth, do you know why no one is around?" I asked her after the first day.

"Yes, Patricia, I do. They have to be carried from place to place."

"I wonder if they really play bridge?" This conversation was taking place over the phone, as Mil and I were completely out of energy after looking at the menu.

The phone call was interrupted by Miss Thin, who informed us that one of the house physicians was ready for the compulsory physical. He carefully took down our histories, checked us from A to Z, and told us we were ready. He explained that after one week of 150 calories we would then be on another type of diet, consisting of 750 calories for two days, and then would go back to 150 for another week. And with that heartwarming bit of information he disappeared to the dining room for a steak. The cook was fabulous, which we only discovered when the men joined us. There they sat eating steak, salad, fresh vegetables, home-baked rolls, and homemade apple pie as Mildreth and I tried to decide whether we would have Column A, B, or C.

The bridge players more or less paralleled the food. Sometimes we would have a fourth from Table A or a third from Table B or a Table C dropout. Faintout was more like it. I tried fainting on the fifth day, didn't like it, never did it again.

The town of Lancaster did provide duplicate bridge for those who had the strength to dress, drive, and sit erect for four hours at a clip. We confined our bridge activity to the inn, as our energy level was low and no one minded if you napped while you were the dummy. Most of the players were congenial and amiable and starving. After a few days of getting acquainted and acclimated, we fell into a regular game. Although our bridge levels differed, our routines and bursts of energy seemed to jibe. This was important because you can't push too hard on such a low-calorie intake and, besides, it's convenient to find others on your body's schedule.

Our regular game would commence after breakfast, which was after weighing, which was before the breakfast we didn't get, which was why we started playing in the morning 'cause we were still hungry from the night before. Anyway, our game consisted of five players (in case someone fainted we were assured of a fourth). The stakes (not steaks — oh, how I yearned for one bite) were moderate and all of the players were as pleasant as one could hope for under the circumstances.

But in the corner of the playing room there was one bigmouth, named Marge. Yakity, yakity, she went all day and night.

"If you had done this" or "If you had done that" or "On page five of Goren's book" — on and on she went. You know the type; there's always one around. I was convinced she had the energy to talk so much because of forbidden food stashed in her room.

As my body shrank from the rapid weight loss, so did my mind. Each time I counted trumps I'd get a different answer. It's kind of embarrassing to have to put the cards down and hold up fingers and toes. Someone suggested a pencil (obviously a friend of Mr. Z.'s — see Chapter 7); however, there is no rule governing fingers and toes.

Our last night at the inn Mil and I were dealt the following hand.

I could see one losing Heart (the Ace), one losing Club (the Ace), and no losing Diamonds. But the Spade situation could be

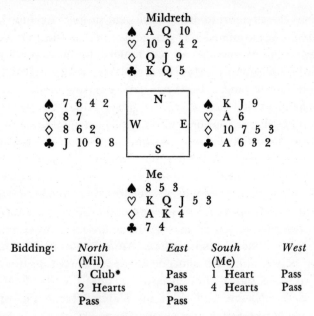

Mildreth
♠ A Q 10
♡ 10 9 4 2
♦ Q J 9
♣ K Q 5

♠ 7 6 4 2
♡ 8 7
♦ 8 6 2
♣ J 10 9 8

♠ K J 9
♡ A 6
♦ 10 7 5 3
♣ A 6 3 2

Me
♠ 8 5 3
♡ K Q J 5 3
♦ A K 4
♣ 7 4

Bidding:	North (Mil)	East	South (Me)	West
	1 Club*	Pass	1 Heart	Pass
	2 Hearts	Pass	4 Hearts	Pass
	Pass	Pass		

All very sane and sensible — considering our condition.
Opening Lead: Jack of Clubs

sticky if both the King and Jack were offside. Sticky is hardly the word — down one better describes it!

We had now been at the farm for two weeks and not only had my poor mind shrunk, but my ability to concentrate was lost somewhere in the Jell-O heap. And Marge, the Tower of Babble, was bellowing across the room. I could hear her complaining about her partner's mistakes, about the food, and once again going through her routine: "First thing I do every morning is strip, then eliminate, and then I —" All of a sudden bigmouth Marge had solved the Spade problem.

"Say it again," I screamed at her from across the room.

"Say what again?" she asked, surprised that someone was listening.

* Convenient minor

"What you do every morning before you weigh yourself."

Befuddled, she repeated, "I strip and eliminate and I —"

Completely forgetting my weakened condition, I sprinted across the room, hugged her wildly, and uttered, "You're really a sensational bridge player." Poor Marge never understood, but her words were the solution to the bridge problem. (Sometimes it even pays to listen to other players' opponents.)

The Jack of Clubs was covered with the Queen, which East won with the Ace. He returned a Club, which was won in the dummy. I then trumped dummy's remaining Club, thus *eliminating* Clubs from both hands. Next came the Jack of Hearts from my hand, which East won with the Ace to return a Heart. Both sides followed so trumps were exhausted. Now comes the *strip*. Before playing a Spade, I cashed the three high Diamonds, ending in my hand. Then I led a low Spade toward the dummy's Ace-Queen-10. When West played low, I put in the 10, which East won.

This is the end position:

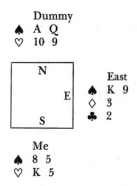

```
           Dummy
        ♠  A  Q
        ♡  10  9

          ┌───────────┐
          │ N         │        East
          │           │     ♠  K  9
          │         E │     ◇  3
          │           │     ♣  2
          │ S         │
          └───────────┘
           Me
        ♠  8  5
        ♡  K  5
```

Any return by East loses a trick for his side. If either a Club or Diamond is returned, simply discard a Spade and ruff in dummy. Obviously, a Spade return assures the finesse. Making 4 Hearts.

The next day Mil and I left the inn quite thin and no longer starving. We had simply forgotten what food tasted like. We arrived home to find the men, in a dear effort to surprise us, had arranged a huge Chinese dinner. Millie took something from Column A, I took something from B, and we made a joint effort on Column C. We bit down on the crunchy noodles, half expecting them to taste like Jell-O.

"Do you miss it?" she asked, obviously reading my mind.

"I'm not sure. Maybe another bite will taste better."

I guess it's like going back to cigarettes. The first one is lousy, the second one a tiny bit better, and the third . . .

"Alfred, please pass the noodles again — and again!!"

Ten courses later we struggled to the bridge table. Mil and I decided we'd play the boys. As a sporting gesture I let her sit South.

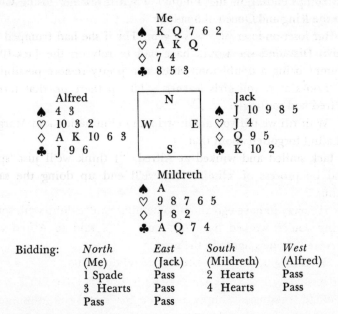

Me

♠ K Q 7 6 2
♡ A K Q
♢ 7 4
♣ 8 5 3

Alfred

♠ 4 3
♡ 10 3 2
♢ A K 10 6 3
♣ J 9 6

Jack

♠ J 10 9 8 5
♡ J 4
♢ Q 9 5
♣ K 10 2

Mildreth

♠ A
♡ 9 8 7 6 5
♢ J 8 2
♣ A Q 7 4

Bidding:	North	East	South	West
	(Me)	(Jack)	(Mildreth)	(Alfred)
	1 Spade	Pass	2 Hearts	Pass
	3 Hearts	Pass	4 Hearts	Pass
	Pass	Pass		

Opening Lead: Diamond King

Alfred led the King of Diamonds, followed by the Ace, and played a third one. Mil just sat still. And stiller and stiller. I was wondering if her mind had shrunk as much as mine. Jack asked her if she was okay and she nodded carefully.

"You know, Pat," she finally answered, "if we keep on eating like we did tonight we're going to be losers all over again."

"I can't argue with that. But it did feel good to eat one meal."

"And," she continued, "there's a time to be a loser on top of a loser and the time is now — at the card table — not at the dinner table."

And with that she discarded a Club from the dummy. She did not trump the third Diamond. Jack won with the Ace, but now the contract was "on ice." He returned a Club, which Mil finessed; she cashed the Ace of Spades and pulled three rounds of trumps ending in the dummy. Then threw her losing Clubs on the King and Queen of Spades.

Her loser-on-loser play was a gem. For if she had trumped the third Diamond she would have had to rely on the Jack-10 of trumps being a doubleton, which is a pretty remote possibility.

"Looks as if you girls learned a lot up there on that farm," Alfred said smilingly.

"Wait till we tell you about strip and elimination and Marge." I hadn't forgotten about that.

Jack smiled and winked at Alfred. "I think we'll just 'split' and by process of 'elimination' we'll end up doing the same thing."

"It's okay to have ego about something you've done well, something you've worked hard for, isn't it?" I said to Alfred as I surveyed my new figure in the mirror.

"That's right," he said as he turned off the lights.

20—

How a Duke Handles Kings and Queens

"SPEND THE WEEKEND playing bridge at the John Waynes'? Are you mad? You know I'm a Democrat."

"They're not interested in your politics, Pat, just your bridge prowess. They're real buffs and anxious to meet you. I'll pick you up in an hour."

In the same breath my friend Joan added, "Bring shore-type clothes and yacht-type clothes . . . the Waynes have a converted minesweeper, *The Wildgoose*. But leave your political party hat home."

There was no denying it; I was excited about meeting the Waynes. Who wouldn't be? Duke is a legend in the industry and it's kicky to see a legend walk and talk. The drive to Newport Beach along the ocean is only an hour from L.A. Joan and I chatted about the house she was renting there for the summer, and I made a mental note to view the house built by Frank Lloyd Wright for Jascha Heifetz many years ago. "You won't have to look hard," said Joan. "It's right across the water from the Waynes'."

"The Amazing Kreskin strikes again! How 'bout saving your mind-reading for the card table?" Joan Blumofe was/is not only a good friend but also a good bridge player . . . as well as a mind reader.

The Wayne house is in a private, well-guarded section of Newport. After identifying yourself at the outer gate, you drive along a road spotted with houses on either side. There is no traffic to speak of, and the children and animals run free. Once inside the Wayne grounds the first thing we saw was the swimming pool, and a few yards past that, the front door of the house, with the fabulous Pilar Wayne framed in the doorway. Immediately you are made to feel welcome by this charming lady from Peru. Pilar is a dark-haired beauty with a divine figure, gorgeous eyes, and a wonderfully warm personality. No wonder the great Duke stumbled from the Pony Express. We seated ourselves in the living room and found ourselves making the usual "Do you know so-and-so?" kind of conversation. (Joan told me later that she was proud of me for not asking, "Let's see, in Washington do you know Dick and Pat Nixon . . . and in Sacramento have you met the Reagans?")

Duke ambled in, just as I had seen him amble a hundred times on film. He gave us big hellos and Duke-size embraces. It takes a few seconds to take all of him in. I've known some big bridge players in my day, but this was a *big* bridge player. He told me that he had played for years and really loved the game. Pilar was an enthusiastic beginner, with many hours of instruction behind her. After I got to know Pilar I learned that whatever she decided to do, she did well. She is a fine tennis player, having started about the same time she started bridge. They have three adorable children running around and one fantastic dog running around with them.

We became friends that first day and have played a lot of bridge since. Never have I heard the Waynes be rude to one another at the table. There were times when they disagreed, but their discussions (at least in front of me) were soft and low-keyed. Fortunately for me, politics never crept into any discussion. It is impossible not to form an opinion when you've heard and read so much about this man. Mine is quite simple. I believe that John Wayne is the product of his screen roles. He has played the All-American — "I love my country" — role for so long that he is what he portrays. It's an honest development, and one to his credit.

Duke won an Academy Award for *True Grit*. As a bridge player, he deserves another Oscar for the grit he displayed on the following deal.

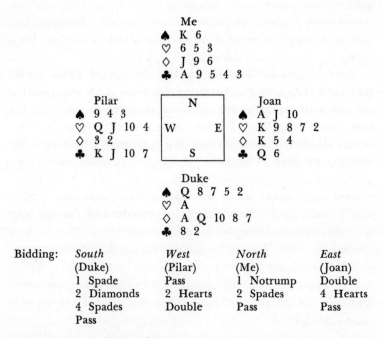

Me
♠ K 6
♡ 6 5 3
◊ J 9 6
♣ A 9 5 4 3

Pilar
♠ 9 4 3
♡ Q J 10 4
◊ 3 2
♣ K J 10 7

Joan
♠ A J 10
♡ K 9 8 7 2
◊ K 5 4
♣ Q 6

Duke
♠ Q 8 7 5 2
♡ A
◊ A Q 10 8 7
♣ 8 2

Bidding:	South	West	North	East
	(Duke)	(Pilar)	(Me)	(Joan)
	1 Spade	Pass	1 Notrump	Double
	2 Diamonds	2 Hearts	2 Spades	4 Hearts
	4 Spades	Double	Pass	Pass
	Pass			

Opening Lead: Queen of Hearts

While Duke pondered the opening lead I pondered Pilar's

double. She was using her own type of grit — mine was confined to the type when the upper back teeth clamp firmly to the lower ones.

Duke won the Heart lead with the Ace and led a small Spade toward the dummy. This was taken by the Ace and another Heart was returned. Duke trumped and laid down the Queen of Spades, followed by another Spade! I held my breath. He saw my face turning light blue as both opponents followed to the Spade lead and said, "Don't worry, little lady, those Spades have got to be thataway."

"I don't know why they have to be thataway. I think the odds are thirty-six to sixty-four that four will be in one hand." My color returned with normal breathing.

Back came another Heart, which he trumped. This left him void in trumps — at a penny a point, doubled. I reached for a drink.

Duke thought for a second, cashed the Ace of Clubs (more grit), and then took the Diamond finesse as if he were putting the last horse in the corral. It never occurred to him that the King would be offside. He gave up a Club trick at the end after he ran all his Diamonds, hoping the opponents would keep the wrong cards. Man, what grit!

"Why didn't you redouble?" he asked me.

"Because I didn't know the Spades were three-three and I didn't know the Diamond finesse was onside, and I'm not sure when grit becomes chutzpah."

I like his style. Just as on the screen, he did his own stunts, took his own chances, and finally was rewarded for both.

The real test of grit came later. We had the most sumptuous Spanish dinner, *paella, pollo al ajillo,* and *natilla.* Duke sat with half of a grapefruit, two hard-boiled eggs, and some salad. It all looked so tiny on the plate next to such a big man. He said that he, like most of us, is always fighting the battle of the bulge, and he diets strenuously before each new film. He stopped smoking years ago after a lung operation, but can drink as every Irishman's reputation says he can drink.

Through the years we played a lot of cards. This legend surely had to have a very special kind of ego, and I waited patiently for it to rear its ugly head. It never happened. John Wayne was given good sturdy looks and an equally sturdy body. He has no need to prove his strength to anybody. He has achieved overwhelming box office popularity and has maintained it for years through hard work and discipline. Newcomers come and go, but Duke goes on and on. He's had his share of health problems, but he never complains — just bitches a bit about diet foods. When my own diet periods coincided with Duke's, we used to have our meals at a card table away from the family and guests. It wasn't as festive, but it was easier than looking at all that gorgeous food.

I remember the first time I used his bathroom. It was an ordinary bathroom with an ordinary sink, tub, toilet, towels — the same as everyone else's. There was John Wayne's toothbrush — the same as yours and mine. He hangs his bathrobe behind the door, too. And he doesn't roll the toothpaste tube either. His hairbrush and comb aren't special in any way. I don't really know what I expected from the bathroom of a man of John Wayne's stature, but I left there feeling it was all rather democratic.

He's raised two families, and now some of his children are the same ages as his grandchildren. This he enjoys immensely. There is always a generation or two of Waynes running around his spacious home. It adds up to a very well-adjusted person, which is exactly what he is at the card table.

Duke Wayne enjoys bridge and plays it well. Like everybody else, he wants to win. He's a good sport, even when he loses — which can't be said about most players. He's a bit reckless, takes chances, and would rather overbid than underbid. As golfers say when they putt: Never up, never in. Bidding three, making four, is not his idea of the game. The only time he gets upset is when his partner stops at a part-score, but this he handles with: "Oh, Golly!" or "Are you sure?" Not that he can't make his language stronger; he just doesn't. He loves pre-emptive bidding. It rouses his spirit and offers a challenge. And as the following hand illustrates, we did not rest in a part-score.

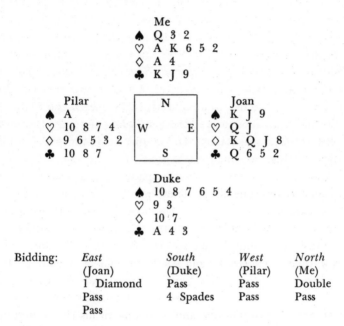

```
                        Me
                    ♠   Q 3 2
                    ♡   A K 6 5 2
                    ◇   A 4
                    ♣   K J 9

    Pilar               N               Joan
♠   A                               ♠   K J 9
♡   10 8 7 4     W           E      ♡   Q J
◇   9 6 5 3 2                       ◇   K Q J 8
♣   10 8 7               S          ♣   Q 6 5 2

                        Duke
                    ♠   10 8 7 6 5 4
                    ♡   9 3
                    ◇   10 7
                    ♣   A 4 3
```

Bidding:

	East	South	West	North
	(Joan)	(Duke)	(Pilar)	(Me)
	1 Diamond	Pass	Pass	Double
	Pass	4 Spades	Pass	Pass
	Pass			

Opening Lead: Diamond 3

Well, you can't say you don't admire his style. I got up to stretch and asked if anyone minded if I looked at my partner's hand. Remember, if you do this you have lost all dummy rights . . . you can no longer keep partner from reneging or playing out of the wrong hand. I almost fainted when I saw our combined trump holding. Duke being strong of heart (weak in Spades) won the lead with the Ace of Diamonds, and as firmly as he grasped that Oscar he led the Queen of Spades. Joan covered with the King (this is the natural thing to do with her holding) and Pilar's Ace fell on top of it. It was quite a clash when the two honors hit, but he knew it was his only chance. The big Wayne grin burst forth. Two more Indians hit the dust. But he still had some handling to do, or lasso the Queen of Clubs, if you prefer. Back came a Diamond from Pilar, which the defense won, then shifted to a Heart. Duke won the Heart with the King, and then his cool, guts, and reasoning took over. He led the Jack of Clubs. Joan had to cover with the Queen and he won with the Ace. His reasoning was correct. West could not have the Club Queen plus the Ace of Spades and pass over partner's opening bid of 1 Diamond. He then played the 2 of Clubs from his hand, West played the 8, and he played the 9 from the dummy. How about that? He wound up losing one Diamond and two Spades, making the game.

"I was afraid you'd pass Three Spades, so that's why I hopped to Four," he offered as an explanation.

"Considering you've only got part of a grapefruit and a hard-boiled egg in your stomach, I don't know where you found the strength to make such a weighty play."

But a pro is a pro on any level. And Duke Wayne is one of the all-time professionals in a rough-and-tough business.

During one of our last games he said he wished he could postpone starting his new film, because location shooting would keep him away for several months and he wanted another week of rest and play. A vice president of United Artists was in the game and remarked, "Well, Duke, if anyone can postpone shooting, certainly you can."

Duke sighed as he shuffled the cards. "Yeah, but if I did it would probably rain the following week and production would really get fouled up." No one said anything. "No." He sighed again. "I'll go and pick up my million on schedule."

I said, "Pass."

21—

The Mad, Mad, Wonderful, Wonderful World of Bridge

WHO'S TO TELL YOU you cannot enjoy a three-dollar bottle of Gallo burgundy but must save up for a thirty-dollar bottle of Lafite Rothschild? Each has its place; each has its own measure of enjoyment. There are times in life when the thirty-dollar bottle would be as out of place as a velvet suit at a picnic.

The wonderful world of bridge is very much the same. I cannot say the games with Omar Sharif and Benito Garozzo were any more enjoyable than the ones with Minnie and Paul or Maxine and Lester. Each had its place and each a special niche in my bidding heart. Had I played with or against Mr. Garozzo way back when, his brilliance would have been completely wasted on my young, inexperienced mind.

The average game at home, which you the public play and enjoy, is the backbone of bridge-playing throughout the world. And it is you and your games most bridge writers hope to reach. As the stars of stage, TV, and cinema rely on the Borscht Belt performers to keep the backbone of show business straight, the so-called biggies in bridge rely on you. You read the columns, buy the books, and are the purchasers of tremendous numbers of playing cards. You make up the huge attendance at bridge tournaments and patronize the local rubber bridge clubs. You are bridge.

Whether you are watching the World Series, the Super Bowl, or the 1976 Olympic games, it is fun to watch the best in the business, to pick up a few hints, and to appreciate why they are the best. So it was when Alfred and I were seated across the table from Benito Garozzo, who is considered by most the best player in the world. He and his Blue Team have won every kind of championship, and each time they step into World Championship competition they take home the blue ribbon.

"Remember," said Alfred, "he is human, and at any single bridge session you and I have as much of a chance or better as anyone else. If we are lucky in getting our share of the cards we will hold our own."

If you find yourself pitted against a better player for an evening, you too can hold your own if you remember to sit tight and do your best. As the cards were dealt I kept reminding myself to be alert and attentive, to bid as accurately as possible, to remember at all times I had a very good partner, Mr. Sheinwold, sitting across the table, and to try to do my best. If you and your partner find yourselves in a similar position, do just that. The bridge expert will not be impressed if you make a flashy bid or play on one hand and then fall on your face the rest of the time, because that is not what bridge is about. It's the constancy and consistency of your game that counts. When playing against Mr. Garozzo I could never convince him that I was the best player in the world, but I could impress him that I wasn't the worst. So can you. Alfred and I have played against many couples who are just average players, but in being consistently average they are good. And in being good they are enjoyable as opponents. And so it was with Benito. He played his usual extraordinary game against us even though he was partnered by a much lesser player.

Benito Garozzo is the co-owner of a jewelry store just off the Via Veneto in Rome. We met him there, did some Christmas shopping, and enjoyed a fantastic meal at his private club before cutting the cards.

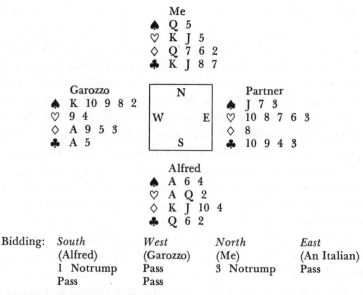

Me
♠ Q 5
♡ K J 5
♢ Q 7 6 2
♣ K J 8 7

Garozzo
♠ K 10 9 8 2
♡ 9 4
♢ A 9 5 3
♣ A 5

Partner
♠ J 7 3
♡ 10 8 7 6 3
♢ 8
♣ 10 9 4 3

Alfred
♠ A 6 4
♡ A Q 2
♢ K J 10 4
♣ Q 6 2

Bidding:

South (Alfred)	*West* (Garozzo)	*North* (Me)	*East* (An Italian)
1 Notrump	Pass	3 Notrump	Pass
Pass	Pass		

Opening Lead: Spade 10

What makes an expert an expert is that he remains expert when all around him are not cooperating — some through ignorance, some deliberately. Mr. Garozzo was sitting West as he watched Alfred rise with the Queen of Spades to win the trick as East played the 7. Alfred played a low Heart to his hand followed by a low Club toward the dummy. For the moment, why not be Mr. Garozzo and make the next play. Don't be too hard on yourself if you played the 5, hoping partner might win with the Queen, thinking partner could then return a Spade through declarer's

Ace-Jack (which you think he holds). Sometimes you are called on to make a quick decision.

But in the West seat sat the best, and up he went with the Ace — because he knew Alfred was *not* finessing for the Queen. The first thing an expert does is to count all the points available to him, and by the time Alfred played the low Club to the dummy, Mr. Garozzo had done his homework — very quickly. He had 11 points, dummy had 12, and Alfred had to have 16. A Queen in his partner's hand would make the grand total 41, which is impossible . . . even in Italy there are only 40 points in the deck. So Benito hopped up with the Ace and continued the Spade suit. Now Alfred had to go down, as the Ace of Diamonds was still against him. A lesser opponent would have ducked the Club; Alfred would have then switched immediately to the Diamond suit and romped home with nine tricks: two Spades, three Hearts, three Diamonds, one Club. Mr. Garozzo's quick, imaginative, and accurate mind defended in his usual style despite the lack of cooperation from his partner. East should have contributed to the defense by playing the Jack on the first trick. This would eliminate any misunderstanding and in turn would be etched much more indelibly on Mr. Garozzo's mind than our failure to make 3 Notrump.

Enjoy your games with better players; do your best, and chances are they will seek you out again. Don't be a smart aleck; don't try to outshine them. You wouldn't try to serve an Ace against Jimmy Connors — you know you can't — but if you keep the ball in play he just might miss. In this case Mr. Garozzo did indeed pick up the ball.

When Mr. Garozzo came to Los Angeles he sought us out. The next time we played a friendly game against him he had a much better partner, Omar Sharif. We had met Omar in 1964 at the second Bridge Olympiad. He was a member of the Egyptian team as well as a nominee for an Academy Award as best supporting actor for his role in *Lawrence of Arabia*. The Egyptian team received a directive prohibiting it from playing against Israel. Mr. Sharif endeared himself to the world of bridge players when, at great risk to his wife and family (still in Egypt), he played a few hands with the Israelis to show where he stood personally. Subsequently he took up residence in France, but at that time he had his neck on the line. The International Board of Governors, called upon to make a ruling, had to stick their necks out and again met the challenge — as they had done over the black issue many years before. Any team wishing to compete in the Bridge Olympiads must play against all countries or withdraw.

Mr. Garozzo is now only a part-time jewelry partner and Mr. Sharif, a part-time actor, as their love of bridge takes up the other part of the time. Together, sponsored by Lancia cars (expensive products of Fiat), they tour the world and challenge bridge teams. Two or three of the other famous Italian Blue Team players make up the balance of this touring team. Any four players wishing to take on Lawrence of Arabia and the Italians may do so and drive home in a new Lancia if they are successful. Personally, I'd rather drive home with either Mr. G or Mr. S.

I found it a little difficult to keep my cool with Omar on my right and Benito on my left, but with Alfred straight ahead of me it was easier.

Naturally, Mr. Garozzo led the suit least preferred by my husband, the declarer. After winning the first trick, Alfred then made the correct play from his hand of the 6 of Hearts. If he could slip one Heart through, he could then switch to the Diamond suit, giving up the King and making the contract. Most players, good or bad, would have ducked the dummy's 10 of Hearts, planning to take it the next time. But Omar was not an ordinary East. His tremendous interest in the game put him in the seat opposite Benito, who in turn sharpened Omar's game to a pinnacle. Omar won the Heart 10 and returned a Club.

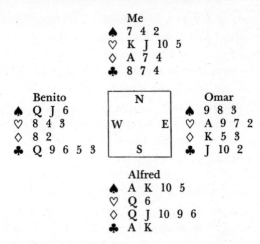

Me
♠ 7 4 2
♡ K J 10 5
◇ A 7 4
♣ 8 7 4

Benito
♠ Q J 6
♡ 8 4 3
◇ 8 2
♣ Q 9 6 5 3

N
W E
S

Omar
♠ 9 8 3
♡ A 9 7 2
◇ K 5 3
♣ J 10 2

Alfred
♠ A K 10 5
♡ Q 6
◇ Q J 10 9 6
♣ A K

Contract: 3 Notrump by South
Opening Lead: 5 of Clubs

He queered Alfred's timing by his own. You must agree it is a pleasure to watch any smooth performance by a good partnership.

"Benito, did you travel thousands of miles just to defeat us again at three Notrump?" I asked him as I wrote down the score.

"Ah, *mia cara*," he replied, "it is so nice to see a husband-wife team go down so graciously."

He knew a lot about graciousness. In Italy he was once trying to console the wife of an American player. The latter had been on the losing team many times even though he was considered the greatest player of his time. Benito found these words to console the distraught wife after the defeat:

"Had there been four of your husband at the table we could never have won."

But the lady was not to be consoled. Instead she kicked Mr. G. in the shins and said, "Fuck you." The next day a dozen roses were delivered from the gracious Mr. G. with a card that read: "When?"

Alfred and I did hold our own with and without the cards. Both times we played against the formidable Mr. Garozzo we picked up some lira and loot. But what I picked up from him at the table could never be measured in money. Next time you feel you are a little over your head, remember, an expert can make you play a little over your head. Experts in anything have a way of making us tighten our belts, heighten our interest, and keep on fighting.

There is one broken card chair in my home, and being a sentimental Leo I'll probably never have it repaired, just increase my personal liability. Alfred thought it should be fixed but he's a man, so how can he look at a chair broken by Rock Hudson with the same eyes as I do?

Mr. Hudson slipped into the chair in question one night at our home as we started a "for fun" twelve-player Individual. We arranged the game using duplicate boards, so all twelve of us would play two hands with each other.

Have you ever noticed Rock Hudson's shy delivery on the screen? You're very much aware that he's there but he doesn't overpower you, even though he's one great big hunk of man. Well, the same quality prevails at the bridge table. I found that I could double him if he was in the wrong contract, but I couldn't use my strongest voice level. Try being the expert around a guy who looks and acts like that when all you want to be is feminine and cuddly. Fortunately for me, the hands we played together were as simple as apple pie, and the ones against him — well, one was lemon and one, lemon-lime — but witness what happened against Alfred.

I was standing behind Joan in full view of Alfred. He gave me an all-knowing look that said: "How did this hand get in here? It's been played before and I know where." I returned his look with: "I thought it would be fun to slip it in for our guests. You didn't have to double." He looked back: "Oh, yes, I did. Fun is fun."

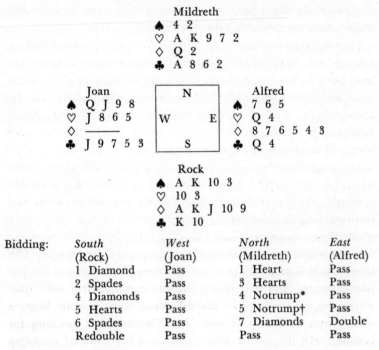

Mildreth
♠ 4 2
♡ A K 9 7 2
◇ Q 2
♣ A 8 6 2

Joan
♠ Q J 9 8
♡ J 8 6 5
◇ —
♣ J 9 7 5 3

Alfred
♠ 7 6 5
♡ Q 4
◇ 8 7 6 5 4 3
♣ Q 4

Rock
♠ A K 10 3
♡ 10 3
◇ A K J 10 9
♣ K 10

Bidding:	*South*	*West*	*North*	*East*
	(Rock)	(Joan)	(Mildreth)	(Alfred)
	1 Diamond	Pass	1 Heart	Pass
	2 Spades	Pass	3 Hearts	Pass
	4 Diamonds	Pass	4 Notrump*	Pass
	5 Hearts	Pass	5 Notrump†	Pass
	6 Spades	Pass	7 Diamonds	Double
	Redouble	Pass	Pass	Pass

Opening Lead: Club 5

Rock just went about his business. After winning the lead, he played two rounds of Spades, then ruffed one Spade with the 2 of Diamonds, heaving a big sigh of relief as Alfred followed to the third round. Then Rock continued his business by cashing his two high Hearts and last high Club, trumping the last Spade with the Queen of Diamonds as Alfred followed forever with his six Diamonds — his six low Diamonds.

When it was all over Rock exclaimed, "I can understand Alfred

---

* Blackwood for Aces.
† Blackwood for Kings; guarantees all four Aces. (Later I asked Mildreth what she would have done had her partner had only two Kings. "Bid six Notrump," she said.)

Sheinwold doubling me, but where I ever got the nerve to bid a slam and then redouble I'll never know."

I guess the answer lies in that funny little thing I keep writing about — ego. Rock was just an amateur in our game, as we would have been in his, but in bridge even the amateur's ego raises its voice and demands to be heard — no matter who you are. But he managed to play a little over his head — just as I had done against Benito Garozzo. Better players can have a good effect on lesser ones — if that ego is in its proper place.

You might look back at the hand Mr. Garozzo defended against us and wonder why I used what appears to be such a simple example. Well, it is the ability to remain consistently alert and constantly disciplined on the mechanical hands that produces a good player. Squeezes, End Plays, and Deschapelles Coups are fun and worth knowing about, but they occur infrequently. The hands dealt time after time, which become routine, are the important ones. And it is your ability to execute them well, time after time, that will make the difference between your being a so-so player and a good one. Mr. Garozzo took nothing for granted. His discipline, which produced his habit of counting each hand and card, led him to the correct play. If you find yourself losing more than you'd like, then you are not handling the routine hands well.

There is tremendous satisfaction in the discipline of bridge as there is in life. And there is great courage in understanding ego. I think Philip, fourth earl of Chesterfield, said it succinctly: "Be wiser than other people if you can, but do not tell them so."

22—

Déjà Vu

"I HATE YOU. I never want to see you again."

Pretty strong words from a past-twenty-year-old to a past-forty-year-old who was neither her father nor her bridge partner. Just her friend.

It wasn't the first time I had felt like a fool at the typewriter, but it was the last time I'd ever let him read my material.

"How could you say that about my story?" I stormed.

"Why did you ask me to read it?" He tried to calm me.

"Because you are an expert and I'm —"

"Talented and inexperienced." He finished the sentence.

I wiped my eyes.

"Pat, do you want to be a good writer?"

"Yes, I do."

"Well, I can help you. But you must be willing to take constructive criticism and instruction without embarrassment . . ."

To the husbands and other men I've played with:

Thanks.